THE
MANAGER
and
THE MONK

JB JOSSEY-BASS™
A Wiley Brand

THE MANAGER
and
THE MONK

A Discourse on Prayer, Profit, and Principles

JOCHEN ZEITZ
ANSELM GRÜN

WILEY

Cover design by Adrian Morgan
Cover image: Copyright © Thinkstock
Originally published in 2010 in German as *Gott, Geld und Gewissen*

English translation by Susan Thorne
Published by Jossey-Bass
A Wiley Imprint

One Montgomery Street, Suite 1200, San Francisco, CA 94104-4594—www.josseybass.com

Jossey-Bass books and products are available through most bookstores. To contact Jossey-Bass directly call our Customer Care Department within the U.S. at 800-956-7739, outside the U.S. at 317-572-3986, or fax 317-572-4002.

Wiley publishes in a variety of print and electronic formats and by print-on-demand. Some material included with standard print versions of this book may not be included in e-books or in print-on-demand. If this book refers to media such as a CD or DVD that is not included in the version you purchased, you may download this material at http://booksupport.wiley.com. For more information about Wiley products, visit www.wiley.com.

Library of Congress Cataloging-in-Publication Data

Library of Congress Cataloging-in-Publication Data has been applied for and is on file with the Library of Congress.

ISBN 9781118479414 (cloth); ISBN 9781118554913 (ebk);
ISBN 9781118555002 (ebk); ISBN 9781118555866 (ebk)

Printed in the United States of America
FIRST EDITION
HB Printing   10 9 8 7 6 5 4 3 2 1

CONTENTS

For Dr. Bernd Deininger with grateful acknowledgment and thanks for his assistance in the development of this book

PREFACE

In choosing to read *The Manager and the Monk*, you have chosen to accompany us on a journey to exchange ideas, challenge long-held belief systems, and discover new possibilities in us all. In fact, you have now become an integral part of this journey of discovery, and as we continue our dialogue, you will foster, deepen, and expand on your own inner dialogue as well.

Our conversation first began in 2008 at an onstage discussion in front of an audience in Nuremberg. As "The Monk" and "The Manager," we faced one another from opposite ends of the spectrum. On one end, Anselm Grün represented a life lived in spiritual practice, and on the other, Jochen Zeitz embodied a life synonymous with business and financial success. On that fateful day we confronted such challenging questions as: Do core values stand a chance in the world of business? To what extent does a monk think like a manager? How much consideration and empathy can a manager afford to show? What do money and success mean to us?

Although we did not have time that day to explore those questions in detail, something intangible but necessary seized us. We were able to gain a basic impression of the other's ideas and instinctively knew that we had happened upon pieces of a puzzle we had both been trying to solve but couldn't finish individually, based just on our own focused and concentrated life experiences. We knew this would be the beginning of another level of enlightenment and knowledge in our lives if we continued our conversation. Since then, we have repeatedly met in person and exchanged e-mails and phone calls. Over time, we developed a unique relationship, one always based on respect and a desire for mutual understanding.

Before our first meeting, we knew a little about each other, thanks to the media:

Anselm Grün was "The Monk," a Benedictine monk from Münsterschwarzach Abbey near Würzburg. He was a renowned author of numerous books on spirituality and counseling and a prominent clergyman. As Cellarer of the abbey, he was responsible for the financial and business management of a community of three hundred monks and staff, overseeing approximately twenty workshops and several hectares of farmland, meadows, and wooded areas.

"The Manager" was Jochen Zeitz, a "citizen of the world" who had, at that time, been chairman and CEO of PUMA, the publicly listed sporting goods and lifestyle company, for eighteen years, since the young age of thirty. The company is headquartered in Herzogenaurach, Franconia, near Nuremberg, and is just 70 kilometers from Münsterschwarzach Abbey. PUMA is a globally recognized brand directly employing over nine thousand employees and providing work for over fifteen thousand people through factories that produce PUMA products. The group has annual sales of over €3 billion.

We were aware that the missions and goals of our organizations and our lifestyles were worlds apart; this is exactly what drew us together. As people—and as authors—we were initially surprised and intrigued to find that there is more that unites us than divides

x

us. We both wish to protect the environment, improve society, and employ sustainable methods, both within our "companies" and beyond. As managers, we must learn to conduct business without harming people or the environment. As spiritual human beings, we look for ways to find ourselves and create more unity without losing sight of the need for efficient management.

During this journey, we did not simply exchange opinions: we also exchanged roles to experience each other's world. The Manager spent some time in the monastery, where he was able to find peace and see his world from a different point of view—and where many things fell into perspective. In return, The Monk expanded his knowledge of "virtual" companies such as PUMA and the fast-paced, electronically networked world of targets and numbers by visiting the group headquarters and attending conferences.

To this day, we continue our exchanges because our main objective is to improve ourselves and our environment, every day and in every way we can. We hope that in reading our book, you too will feel encouraged and inspired to seek the same goal and open your world and mind, continuing our conversation within yourself.

Anselm Grün and Jochen Zeitz

THE
MANAGER
and
THE MONK

CHAPTER 1

SUCCESS

WITH AN INTRODUCTION BY
JOCHEN ZEITZ

When I was asked to take over the helm of PUMA at twenty-nine, I inherited a company nearing bankruptcy. Three CEOs had failed in the previous three years and the company had lost money for eight consecutive years. In my first two years at PUMA, the company had nothing to show in terms of success. During this time I felt tremendous happiness when at least our athletes won. Following drastic cost-cutting measures, the only three well-known athletes whom I had been able to keep under sponsoring contracts all won gold medals in the 1992 Olympic Games in Barcelona. Years later I had the same feeling of deep satisfaction when Serena Williams, one of our PUMA athletes, rose up in the tennis world and became the first African-American to lead the world rankings. I was glad four years ago when Italy—sponsored by PUMA—unexpectedly won the world championship after a sensational scandal in the Italian soccer league.

I was just as pleased about Usain Bolt, whom we had put under contract as a seventeen-year-old. Winning the Olympic gold medals for the 100-meter and 200-meter sprints in *both* Beijing in 2008 and London in 2012, Bolt has often been dubbed "the fastest man

1

ever." Running against other mortals Bolt does give the impression of moving so fast that he could reach liftoff and fly. And he has become all but a superhero to his fellow Jamaicans—he won half of their Olympic gold medals in both 2008 and 2012. Bolt, whom I have been privileged to know since he became affiliated with PUMA, had been written off by many track experts when he was injured, and when he seemed not serious about training early on in his career. Others sometimes encouraged me to drop him as one of our PUMA athlete representatives. And yet I stood behind him as he set world records again and again. Bolt has always rebounded from setbacks to become even faster. This triumph over the odds raises the bar for what is possible in the realms of national and personal athletic success.

Whenever PUMA has been associated with an outstanding athletic moment through the victories of excellent athletes, my team and I were successful. We felt pride, joy, and happiness—all at once.

THE SUCCESS PYRAMID

It is usually triumphs like these, whether our own or those of people with whom we are associated, that stamp our concept and understanding of success. There is a Success Pyramid corresponding to the American psychologist Abraham Maslow's Hierarchy of Needs Pyramid. Maslow explained the goals of human action in 1943 by means of the model of steps: different important human needs make up the steps of a pyramid that the individual climbs. First, he strives to satisfy his physical needs: food, warmth, clothing, reproduction. Once he succeeds in this, he searches for safety, then later on for social belonging, personal recognition, and finally self-actualization.

The level of each person's success also depends on his or her personal values and standards for success. Those for whom competitions, personal-best accomplishments, and unmatched excellence play a great role will perhaps regard a gold medal at the Olympic Games as the highest measure of success. Others place value on cooperation, sympathy, and creative solutions.

In today's consumer society, those people who have more euros, dollars, or yuan at their disposal are considered more successful. Mantras such as "more is better," "size matters," and "quantity, not quality" drown out the call for more profound definitions of success.

I don't want to give the impression that I consider material success unimportant. I personally appreciate prosperity because along with it come greater freedom, independence, and choices. Specifically, I have a growing number of opportunities to devote myself to tasks outside my profession, to experiment, and to realize my dreams in these areas. Thus, I would certainly not say that money is the root of all evil, but I will say that when someone primarily wants to make gold and accumulate it at any price, it is unlikely that he will behave correctly, responsibly, or unselfishly. For me, this is all a matter of balance and harmony, but this does not mean refusing material things in favor of spiritual ones, or the reverse. It is valid instead to appreciate both, recognizing that they complement each other. Victories and gestures of humanity do not exclude each other. Sometimes the first of these just makes the second one possible!

Maslow's pyramid begins at the bottom with the fundamental, bodily, existential needs. Materialism plays the decisive role here. Millions of people chalk it up as a success when they just survive one more day or one more year. Food, clothing, and other material goods are much more important for those who never have the luxury of taking them for granted. But is this minimum or maximum success? It doesn't appear to be an earth-shattering triumph when one has to be content just to survive or merely to exist. For an existentialist, however, being happy and pleased to exist is a success.

As a manager at PUMA, I have definitely reached the highest rung of success; in Maslow's model, I have been striving for self-actualization for a long time. Yet needs arise even at this level, and the way you define your success changes. In the beginning, I felt that I was successful when I managed to renew the company in a tricky situation, step by step. I was enormously satisfied that I could help more and more people get jobs and positions and offer customers better performance. But over time, I raised the measuring yardstick higher and higher. Record wins were supposed to be achieved in unbroken succession, for as many years as possible.

Then I strove for creative success, and we triumphed when we became the first sports lifestyle brand. We sounded a paradigm shift in our sector by combining sport, an attitude to life, and fashion. Every innovation that our company designed seemed to me to be a higher form of success, a higher prize to tick off. It became important to be ahead in our sector and to keep redefining our brand. To me, our recognition as an innovative, rule-changing company felt like a new form of success.

Our idea of success changes with age, experience, and awareness. Today I strive for success in going beyond conventional company management. One success along the way was PUMAVision, which we developed. Another is my private foundation, which is intended to make a contribution to nature conservation.

HAVING OR BEING

The psychologist Erich Fromm didn't ask, "To be or not to be?" but rather "To have or to be?" In his book by the same name, Fromm puts forward the thesis that there are two types of existence quarreling over the soul of man. On one side, the power called "having" pulls us toward accumulation of power and possessions—the trappings of traditional success—and ultimately in the direction of the aggression necessary to attain them. This dark power is embodied in global violence, avarice, and envy. On the other side, the force of "being" pulls us toward love and the joy of sharing and creating. This "being" leads to productive activity and to creative relationships supporting the best in a society.

In a similar fashion, Martin Buber differentiated between "being" and "appearing." A large part of our human struggle for survival, Buber says, has to do with the striving for a particular appearance. We want to impress, so instead of being ourselves, we wear masks to give us a certain appearance while we actually lead a hidden life. These are not masks in the form of makeup, clothing, or rituals behind which we hide our bodies, as for Carnival or Halloween; but rather the pretenses, justifications, and even lies with which we hope to conceal our authentic selves. "Appearing" keeps us from reaching the goal of "authenticity," as Buber calls it—but all too often the rules of traditional success value appearances over authenticity.

Can a person truly be successful when he no longer is present enough to smell the fragrance of roses, taste the flavor of coffee, or feel every drop of water in a shower? Psychologists maintain that we miss two-thirds of our lives because we spend one third of every moment in the imaginary future and another third in the past. We ask ourselves what our neighbor meant with his comment yesterday, and torment ourselves about whether the person of our desires will call—and in the process, we miss the sunset taking place directly before our eyes, and forget to live. Presumably true presence in every single moment, or more precisely just "being," is at the very top of the Success Pyramid.

Many managers suffer from a syndrome that could be called "push-aholism"—that is, the constant pressure to look ahead and get ahead. "Push-aholism" can eventually lead to burnout. Often I catch myself racing around in overdrive, forgetting to observe life's rhythms, to have regular moments of relaxation, or to set work aside on Sundays. I know that this also puts a strain on my colleagues. I know that in all the years of my striving to help PUMA get ahead, I have not paused often or long enough to quietly enjoy my successful moments with my team and my family. I have been pleased in private, but I always felt pressure to start working immediately on the next task, instead of appropriately acknowledging the people who shared success with me and letting them have some much-needed rest. I know now that better balance is important.

When I became the head of marketing at PUMA, another individual lost his job. My success underlined the failure of another person. And when I became CEO and chairman of the board, I had to dismiss former colleagues who didn't conform to my vision of a successful future for PUMA. From their perspectives, they were thwarted in their careers at PUMA, while I was successful in my own view. We should always be aware of the effects of our decisions.

SUCCESS IN A GROUP

Are individuals or a group most likely to achieve the greatest possible success? This question deserves examination because, on the one hand, a manager can influence the lives of many customers, shareholders, colleagues, employees, salespeople, and suppliers. On the other hand, a manager's personal success depends significantly on the success of his team or the company family—just as team athletes learn early on that personal success by itself does not lead to a shared victory. For this reason we want to strengthen our commitment to ethics, responsibility, arts, the environment, and society, aided by our PUMAVision. The entire business world should work more closely toward this goal alongside social groups and institutions, and not focus exclusively on financial profits. Business is a part of society and the environment in which all sectors are connected with each other and with the greater whole. To support the environment means supporting one's own self. So it should be in the enlightened interest of each individual to pursue and cultivate a collegial if not spiritual attitude to focus on the greater, higher whole.

We could establish indicators for companies that integrate environmental and social issues, such as the Gross Sustainability Index, or better still, the Global Sustainability Index. For some time, there have been attempts to measure collective success at the national level. Bhutan's former King Jigme Singye Wangchuck, who wanted to maintain the Buddhist values of his country and define quality of life in a holistic manner (and not just in terms of the gross national product), coined the concept of "Gross National Happiness." The core of this notion is the idea that real prosperity results when spiritual and material development complement and strengthen each other.

There is a similar economic concept described as the General Progress Indicator (GPI). The GPI indicates economic and ecological welfare, and can replace the Gross Domestic Product (GDP) as a standard for economic growth. With the GPI, economists and politicians are trying to measure whether growth in goods and services really leads to greater well-being and prosperity among citizens.

Not only does the idea of collective success generate new statistical data, but it also leads to new models, such as the "Win-Win Model" of Bill Ury and Roger Fisher, experts in negotiation and authors of the book *Getting to Yes*.[1] Instead of postulating that one person's success inevitably brings harm to others, they have developed a model that allows both or even multiple sides to win. This win-win approach starts with the assumption that several parties pursuing different goals can agree on a higher, shared purpose rather than engaging in conflict. Applied consistently, this bargaining discipline will lead to a solution that satisfies all participants. This model has often been put into practice successfully—between employers and employees, and between competing companies or governments.

This prototype is diametrically opposed to the model of winning at any price, which drives many companies, careers, and athletes. It thus avoids the serious disadvantages of the winner-loser model, which are very well illustrated by another sporting event: the so-called "Underarm Incident," which took place in 1981 during the third of five games in the final round of the cricket world championship in Australia. In that game, Australia, the host country, deprived the New Zealand team of the chance to even up the score by having the Australian bowler roll the ball over the grass (using what is called an "underarm delivery") toward his opponent instead of throwing it. This technique was certainly legal, but it was regarded as highly unsportsmanlike, and was later forbidden by the International Cricket Council. The Australian team won the match in this way and became world champions, but the team lost its good reputation. The Australian cricket team was driven off the field by booing from the astonished spectators. The team's short-term success ended with long-term damage to its image.

Following the Enron and Lehman Brothers scandals, companies are starting to search for new models of success. Leadership paradigms like the ones put forward by David Strauss at Harvard[2] and Peter Senge of MIT[3] have inspired many CEOs to bet on cooperation instead of confrontation. The Strauss-Senge leadership paradigm says that success can have both a personal and collective character at the same time; that is, you can achieve personal goals together with other like-minded executives. Managers can be connected in a larger network with people who work for goals that may benefit the entire planet—the environment and society. Some people maintain that real personal success must be collective in character. In this way, such success is elevated to a higher step on the pyramid.

PERSONAL SUCCESS

Having brought out many merchandise collections, ideas, and concepts over the past twenty years, my highest priorities today are things that are good for my own self, for nature, and for society. I don't want to downplay my personal goals, for of course I have them like anyone else. But my concept of personal success has always included standing with both feet planted firmly on the ground, in a state of balance with my inner self. In my eyes, an important element of personal success is recognizing and understanding more deeply what make me the person I am. My success calls for constant development, expanding my consciousness, deepening my thinking. I endeavor to accept my own shortcomings and the imperfections of others, to learn how to deal with life's difficult questions, and to preserve a positive attitude in the process. I have learned how important it is to enjoy the highs and at the same time understand that the lows are a part of life that brings insight. Success for me also means respecting myself and the story of my own life—the happy as well as the less happy days.

After all, success is not just measured in triumphs, but also in how we face up to and overcome limitations.

I am grateful for Usain Bolt and others who inspire us to overcome our limitations, to speed like lightning and to fly to the finish. Ultimately, I wish such success not only to our readers but also, as you will see in later chapters, to the entire planet.

DIALOGUE: MANAGER AND MONK

ANSELM GRÜN: For me personally, being outwardly recognized as successful is not the most important thing. Instead, success for me means being able to realize my intentions through the things that I do. Success comes from following. When my actions follow my ideas and convert them into deeds, then that is success for me. An important criterion for success is working efficiently so that I have as little wasted energy as possible in my work, and achieve my goal with minimal resources.

Efficiency has two aspects for me. The first is a spiritual one: I work efficiently when I am totally involved in an activity and not expending too much energy on secondary objectives. These secondary concerns might include the constant striving for good assessments, recognition, and acknowledgment. If I am always thinking about whether others will appreciate my work enough, then I am not concentrating, and I progress more slowly and use more energy. This is not working in an energy-efficient way—it is a waste of energy. This spiritual aspect applies not only to my personal work but also to the work of a company. Often too much energy is squandered because employees don't respect each other's dignity and constantly degrade each other. Instead of being pleased about the abilities of others and using them, coworkers sometimes hold back good employees, preventing them from looking good or having too high an opinion of themselves. Spirituality means being pleased about the dignity of coworkers and supporting their capacities, to the benefit of individuals and the whole.

The second aspect of efficiency is organizing my work so that I can accomplish as much as possible in the shortest possible time. That means not just leaving work procedures as they are, but observing them and considering whether they are still practical. It is helpful to use employees' experiences here, for they often have a sense for what could make their work simpler, clearer, and more transparent.

However, efficiency mustn't become a "golden calf" to which you pray, or it will become a curse for the company. Sustainable efficiency requires thinking about nature. Nature grows efficiently, but this efficiency is not limitless. It corresponds to the intrinsic nature of plants. We work efficiently, then, when we are in harmony with our own inner being and with nature. If we imitate nature well, we will continually refine the art of living and organize it more effectively.

JOCHEN ZEITZ: Even as a CEO, I agree with you: work doesn't always need to be more efficient. In the final analysis, you can make the wrong things more efficient in the wrong way! Managers and monks acknowledge successes that help us to learn from each other and inspire each other. As a manager, I was impressed with the all-inclusive sustainability of the monastery: its social, ecological, commercial, and, of course, meditative success. I was also touched by the living harmony, the sincerity, and the positive attitude of the people there. But I also think that monks who have come to know the core of a well-run company are somewhat amazed at the resources, the effectiveness of the public relations, the breadth and productivity of fully developed business practices.

When we apply the concept of efficiency to our planet and to nature, and when we look at ourselves and how we employ our resources, then we realize that we must drastically improve our efficiency through higher productivity in resource use. In order to achieve this, we need creative and constructive procedures that will enable us to achieve our work results more efficiently. And these procedures must also bring about changes in our current business systems and our products through innovation and redesign, so that we will be organized for a new, sustainable model.

11

Efficiency is just one of many competing goals in a business system, after all. Different definitions of efficiency can complement or stand in contradiction to each other. Efficiency is most frequently contrasted with morality, particularly with the concepts of freedom, justice, and preserving nature. However, these do not necessarily apply at each other's expense.

The basic approach in the business world concerns creating services and fundamentals for living, and as a result I believe that earning money and doing good are not opposed to each other. You can earn money as a company by doing good. Today there are more and more successful companies that contribute to cleaning up the environment or educating others about it, instead of harming it. As an example, you can earn money by offering more accurate weather reports that provide better warnings about impending hurricanes, snowstorms, and tsunamis. Dedication to the general public doesn't necessarily lead to less profit; it could just as well lead to prosperity based on a new business and industrial paradigm. Because our business model must change radically in favor of a more secure, cleaner, and more peaceful world (and will, I believe), innovative and dynamic companies and entrepreneurs will find countless opportunities to do justice to this task. Businesses will be set up and organized around economic sustainability, with a long-lasting, sound base in terms of earnings and prosperity; and they will simultaneously conserve our environment and its natural resources. In this way, economic growth at any price will be replaced by sustainable growth.

PUMA's products don't enhance environmental protections, yet our shareholders know that we are committed to create value in the long term, and that sustainability in every respect is anchored in our vision, mission, and positioning. Consequently, actions against ecological and social sustainability would simply mean acting against the interests of our company, our brands, our values, and also our own shareholders. In all my years at PUMA, I have always believed in the concept of long-term shareholder value and acted accordingly. With this approach, sustainability and shareholder value are compatible in the long run, even if we must invest first to reach our goals regarding sustainability.

ANSELM GRÜN: Sustainability for me doesn't only mean dealing with the resources of Creation in a sustainable way and protecting the environment. We should also handle our own powers in a sustainable fashion, and the powers of our employees. It is also a matter of social sustainability—a sustainable relationship with our coworkers and their resources.

Regarding the first of those, it includes the protection of workplaces. This can run counter to efficiency, for companies today are making massive cuts in their personnel costs. However, the art of management consists of organizing everything so that employees will gladly carry out their assignments, and will know their role in the firm, the influence they can exert, and their creative power. The executive doesn't have to have everything under his or her control, but should arrange the firm's internal systems so that tasks and competencies are clearly defined, and employees like working there. You cannot have good workplace relations unless clarity prevails. There are different leadership styles, of course. One person might set goals and try to communicate them; another proceeds more by systematic thinking and tries to shape the community to become outwardly fruitful in its work while wasting little effort internally. But without leadership, no society will be able to thrive in the long run or cooperate in a lasting way.

The principles that you illustrated with examples from sports also apply to monks and managers: it is not important to be first all the time. The path of holiness does not begin at my door. As Cellarer, I don't have to know exactly about everything; I don't have to be the best bookkeeper, the best organizer, the best tax adviser, the best finance manager. I also don't have to be the most complete or most spiritual monk. Nonetheless, a Cellarer and an abbot are needed in a monastery, just as a business needs a manager. Even in monasteries, one has the illusion that small communities need no authority and that they can lead themselves. But that's a mistake because where there is no clear structure, informal power structures will develop on their own. Then the most assertive Brother will assume leadership, but if his power is not clearly established, he will only exercise it when doing so benefits him. When he is supposed to assume responsibility for the community, however, he will refuse and draw back so that he has no official leadership role. Such unclear power structures are not good for either the community or a firm.

JOCHEN ZEITZ: Management is necessary: we all need coordination to carry out our tasks, regardless of whether we assume the best or the worst about people. When people are good, in keeping with their basic nature, they still need someone to coordinate their efforts—just as a conductor leads good musicians in an outstanding orchestra. But even when we are egotistic and selfish, we need a director who can motivate us to practice independently of each other, and keep us from throwing our instruments at musicians we do not like.

14

For executives, this means leading by providing a good example; then those who are good by nature will follow, and those who have a rather negative character will be drawn along by the stream of those who take the executive's integrity as a model. It is important for managers to keep integrity in mind, regardless of whether employees yield to their strengths or to their weaknesses.

In the course of our lives, all of us will probably have our strengths as well as our weaknesses come to light. When managers support the best procedures and ethical standards and, using their highest abilities, set a living example of these, then they have great influence and can also bring out the ideal side of others. We have all made mistakes, and we managers too are by no means perfect, of course, so it is good that we have ethical guidelines—not to mention our supervisory boards, governing bodies, and the public, who keep an eye on us.

ANSELM GRÜN: A manager doesn't have to be perfect, but if he makes a public claim about something that isn't the case, he will encourage this kind of behavior in his employees, too. On the other hand, when the manager is true to himself and his weaknesses, this will create a workplace climate in which each person is thankful for his strengths, but can also admit and talk about his weaknesses. That doesn't mean that we all have to belittle ourselves and make excuses for our many weaknesses. It is a question more of openness and calmness, not fooling anyone, and creatively handling weaknesses as well as strengths.

I don't have the right to demand that all employees follow my instructions, but I do have the right to discuss this with them. If they believe that my instructions don't make sense for them, then they must give reasons and we can look into changing the instructions. As manager, I can also learn from my employees. But on no account can I just give in because many instructions appear to be unenforceable. If the employees don't convince me to change policy, then it's up to me to see that they do what I have instructed, in harmony with others in the responsible group. Struggling for solutions stimulates interaction, but finding solutions takes clear decisions, too—above all when there is no consensus among the employees. My duties will be better implemented when employees have confidence that I have not decided arbitrarily, but by listening to my own voice as well as the voice of God. I cannot say, "I hear God's voice, so you must do as I say." Then I would be putting myself above others. Nobody can claim God's voice for himself alone. That is nothing but an attempt to predict God's voice by listening to one's own soul. God's voice expresses itself in clarity, freedom, enthusiasm, and peace. Benedict reminds us that we should hear God's voice in the stillness, but also hear Him by listening to other Brothers and employees.

JOCHEN ZEITZ: In the end, people define professional and private success and the meaning of their actions in their own very personal ways. When I fully retire, my idea of my success will presumably center around having created a space with a positive effect on people—a creative, supportive, and helpful space. Looking back, I would be glad to be able to say, as George Bernard Shaw expressed it, that my life was one that burned like a torch rather than a candle.

The Buddhist outlook on life, in which there is no ultimate sense of life but only life itself, appeals to me personally. We jump into the river of life, experience beauty and excitement, and do our best. Finally, regardless of other uncertainties, there is always the certainty that we can now live this one life.

I am not concerned with reaching a complete, quantitatively measured level of success or exhausting my full potential. I am more interested in appreciating the journey of life itself and being satisfied with it. I see myself as a small drop in the ocean of the universe. But even a drop leaves traces behind, however infinitely small these may be. If I can be sitting in a rocking chair someday in the future with a smile on my face, this will mean that I have had a good and fulfilled life, including the part referred to as my "career."

ANSELM GRÜN: When I give up my work as Cellarer to younger Brothers, I won't measure success by whether they continue to do things just like me. They may well emphasize different aspects in their management capacity. My work will have been a success if I can look thankfully back on my time as Cellarer, if my coworkers remember me with pleasure, and if important ideas that I put in place have continuing value. I will chalk it up as a success if I can let go of my work and turn myself with my whole heart to the other duties that will be important for me then. For I will not sit in a rocking chair after my time as Cellarer. I will instead do what my heart urges me to do. I will have more time for reading and writing, for carrying on conversations and keeping company with people. Everything that I have done so far should accompany me later in my new activities. Then I will feel in harmony with myself. That is success for me.

CHAPTER 2

PROSPERITY

WITH AN INTRODUCTION BY
ANSELM GRÜN

The Bible tells us that God wants humankind to do well on earth, and to be prosperous enough to live in peace and find happiness. In the eight Beatitudes, Jesus described an eightfold path—similar to the Buddha's eightfold path—for the achievement of happiness and success in life, but He doesn't promise us an ideal world. Man will only be happy if he lives in harmony with himself and his lot, if he is fair to himself and his fellow men, and free of dependencies. If Man is ruled by God rather than his own ego, then he will be truly free and will become the kind of human being God created.

Saint Benedict established a clear Rule organizing monastic life along these lines. The Rule focuses on both spiritual and physical health: Benedict emphasizes a healthy daily rhythm corresponding to the human biorhythm, and a proper balance of eating, praying, and working. This "wise moderation" is the ultimate virtue for him: it helps the monk to lead a successful life and contributes to his well-being, but it also involves his renouncing the life of luxury. Benedict belongs to the ascetic tradition in monasticism. For him, asceticism means achieving inner freedom through constant practice. The remarkable thing is that the very communities which practiced this asceticism not only lived in a healthy manner but also achieved a certain outer prosperity. The Cistercian monasteries, which strongly emphasized asceticism, are the best example of this, having been among the wealthiest monasteries of the Middle Ages. This development is also apparent in economic history: those financially successful elites that shaped society were always ascetic elites.

When Ludwig Erhard was Germany's first minister of economic affairs in the postwar period, he promised the Germans prosperity. After all their privations in the wake of two world wars, prosperity was something that people longed for. The word denoted a state of overall well-being: freedom from uncertainty about having a livelihood, and the freedom from want that this assures. But financial prosperity alone is not sufficient for human well-being; it also requires good social interaction, security, prospects for the future, and the feeling that one's own life has meaning.

You also need health. Health is the highest priority for many people today, and for many individuals, it has become an outright substitute for religion. Yet an exclusive preoccupation with your own health can make you ill. The history of monastic living shows that a healthy lifestyle includes appropriate moderation and a strong grounding in religion. Religious rites and practices support health. Even the Greeks knew that human beings are only healthy when they live commensurate with their own state of being. "Religio," connectedness to God, is an important component of this.

In the 1970s, the expression "affluent society" was used rather negatively. There was a feeling that people were too fixated on material things and ignored other values, that they consumed too much and were falling into a particular kind of lethargy. In an affluent society many certainly feel well, but may not be contributing to society, laying the groundwork for a mentality of taking rather than giving. After the Second World War, achieving a certain level of prosperity was regarded as a goal worth striving for. People devoted all their energies to building their own houses, making arrangements for the future, and indulging in a pleasant life. The children of this generation, the baby boomers, thought it would continue like this, always progressing upward, without any exertion on their part. They were sated and lethargic, and had forgotten that we have to work for prosperity. We must learn anew that we have to work for our well-being. This is true for industry and commerce but also for our personal development. There is no life without struggle and exertion. But if that struggle is reduced to a struggle for prosperity, then there simply is no prosperity at all.

In the Christian tradition, poverty has been extolled as something desirable. Jesus himself calls those who are poor "blessed." The Buddhists speak of nonattachment; Jesus spoke of the same thing. Neither prosperity nor wealth should be valued as negative in themselves, only the dependency on them. C. G. Jung maintained that affluence has a tendency to amplify a person's mask, and can cause that individual to cut himself off from his soul and center his life entirely on money and riches, with the result that he becomes empty within.

In the so-named mendicant orders, poverty has now been elevated to an ideal. It is not a question of inner freedom from things but of outer poverty; members of the order deliberately live without any possessions to demonstrate their solidarity with the poor. Saint Benedict does not recognize this type of poverty. He speaks of a community of property where monks own everything in common. That is supposed to free the individual from becoming dependent on objects. But this can also lead to a prosperity that suppresses the spiritual life. For this reason Benedict connects the community of property with economy and simplicity. A monk's life should be simple, and it requires ongoing, honest self-searching to discover whether one has become too dependent on a certain standard of living.

The promotion of poverty, on the other hand, can sometimes lead to a denial of life: one no longer allows oneself anything and has a bad conscience about wanting to enjoy something

21

or possessing certain property. This results in valuing money as something fundamentally negative. Benedict understands this differently. He maintains that the monastery should have a certain degree of prosperity—enough to surround the sacred spaces with a certain splendor, for instance. Uncompromising poverty leads to a lack of culture. Both prosperity (and an inner freedom regarding it) and nonattachment are needed in order to concentrate on the real goal of humankind: God.

DIALOGUE: MANAGER AND MONK

JOCHEN ZEITZ: There is a general human tendency to give value and credibility only to those things that can be counted. We have continually found more and more ways to buy and sell values and their copies. We need to go beyond this purely quantitative approach and look into ourselves with open eyes to find meaning, purpose, and other standards for measuring prosperity.

If we human beings were to step back briefly from our daily business and its associated pressures, almost all of us would say that we recognize and value many forms of prosperity, such as happiness, health, learning, and nature. When it comes to the things that we value, we are alike in many respects, yet we are socially conditioned to privilege our differences over our shared interests. I believe that we live and experience a prosperity that goes beyond the material realm.

ANSELM GRÜN: Every individual longs to live with a certain measure of prosperity. But that may no longer be enough for someone who wants to own more and more property. That person will be plagued by anxiety about defending his possessions against others. This is graphically clear in South America, for example, where the rich have to erect walls around their estates in order to set themselves apart from the poor of society, and secure and defend their prosperity. Rather than enjoying their prosperity, they live in constant fear that it could be stolen. The individual who totally dedicates himself to external prosperity becomes insatiable. He will never have enough.

Jesus addressed this human longing for prosperity in his teachings, but He directed it inward: the true riches of Man are in his soul. Jesus speaks metaphorically about treasure in the fields and costly pearls, and about the things that give humanity real dignity and radiance. These are found in the beauty of Man's soul, which expresses itself in clarity, love, light, freedom, and peace.

Prosperity, as the word indicates, is a condition: I am in a state of feeling well and healthy and content. Success, on the other hand, is the result of an action, the attaining of a goal; it always depends on my making an effort. But even success can become an end in itself. When that happens, I will be incessantly driven by the pressure to be even more successful, rather than reflecting proudly on what I've attained. Many people define themselves entirely in terms of this value: they are only really alive when they are successful. Yet all too often they break down when success fails to materialize. Genuine prosperity and a true feeling of wellness don't result from outer success, however, but from inner agreement within myself and joy in the values that make my life worthwhile.

JOCHEN ZEITZ: Every person has to find a balance between material and nonmaterial prosperity. Society is not permitted to distinguish between money and the spirit based on a division of labor. In some cases, businesses still feel that it is the church's exclusive job to take people in and concern itself with their spiritual and psychological welfare, whereas a company's sole duty is to earn money.

In the developed nations, I think we are reaching the end of the era of traditional industrialization, with its emphasis on economic growth aimed at purely material prosperity. This kind of industrial expansion has passed its peak, because resources are running out and we have overstepped the natural limits and the long-term, natural carrying capacity of the ecosystem. Furthermore, part of that growth is not true growth but should be considered artificial, as the subprime financial as well as Euro crisis have proven so impressively. These facts are leading more and more managers to consider change.

The laws of nature are coming into play. Even if you can print money to save a bank, you still can't print life to save a planet. You have to honor the sacredness of life. Religion and the economy both have a job to do in this regard.

The ideal of prosperity must be looked at in a fresh way and developed further. So far as the material side of prosperity is concerned, the new ideal should be based on an innovative and evolved industrial paradigm that improves social standards and heals our sick Earth at the same time. Because wind and solar power are renewable forms of energy, these can create a novel prosperity—particularly in developing countries—while simultaneously contributing to this new model of industrialization. But we need a shifting and changing of values and rules to underpin this displacement and the changes in the economy. In other words, we can no longer focus only on the significance of capital, but must also refer to the sanctity of life.

Within this changing paradigm, we must learn to live happily in prosperity without reference to the purely materialistic definition of happiness. We need a new qualitative growth based on a new model of happiness and prosperity. I would like to mention that the Rocky Mountain Institute in the United States has put forward an alternative view of this kind by stating that prosperity does not have to be based on growth. Indeed, the institute maintains that many problems confronting communities today have actually resulted from growth.

All this means that not only religion but the economy, too, must make humankind and nature its concern. The economy may have another focus, but happiness, health, and satisfaction in the workplace should be goals for managers, in addition to their business duties.

ANSELM GRÜN: If the Church were the sole caregiver for victims of rigid economic policies, this would sanction a system that would not be good for people in the long run. Companies must facilitate an employment working climate in which people will gladly participate. Being able to work well is essential to human health. And the converse is true: fulfilling work contributes to health. Religions have the job of reminding companies again and again of their duty to care for people. Companies that treat their employees well and create a healthy working atmosphere will have greater success in the long run. That doesn't mean that companies should exploit religion to achieve greater success. But business and religion can supplement each other.

Religions show business what is sacred to people. I am pleased that you, Mr. Zeitz, have alluded to the sanctity of life. *Sanctity* is a religious term. I have also seen it in a book about the culture of leadership. Lance H. K. Secretan,

25

a Canadian corporate consultant, talks about how we should make the company into something sacred.[1] By this he means that people's workplaces are environments where they recognize their own dignity, where they not only work but philosophize with others, develop new ideas, let their souls take flight. For the Greeks and Romans, the sacred was that which is withdrawn from the world—that over which the world has no power. Only when the business world pays attention to the sacredness of life and humanity, when it no longer completely monopolizes humankind, using people for financial purposes—only then will business settle its account fairly in terms of human dignity, and the sanctity of life and nature.

The Christian religion took over the "art of healthy living" from Greek philosophy and medicine, and supported and enlarged it to give humans healing rituals. Rituals create a sacred time, a time which belongs solely to me and God. That is true for the personal rituals which I carry out myself in order to remain myself in the face of all my professional challenges. This is also valid for the rituals in a firm. Company rituals show what one thinks of people and their dignity.

Through rituals, a holy space and holy time come into being—even in the middle of the working world—which create a healing atmosphere. Then something new dawns in the company which is greater than itself, and in this way religion and business can complement each other. Business can learn much from the religions about permanently achieving good interaction between working individuals, to the benefit of the people and finally also to the benefit of the firm. Religion keeps space open for God—for something greater than man—in this society. And only in this broader horizon of God will man live

26

freely in the long run. When society becomes completely settled in its ways and does not keep alive its yearning for what is completely different, it will take on totalitarian characteristics and want to control humanity absolutely. But that is not good for anyone. Religion is the guarantor of enduring freedom for humankind.

JOCHEN ZEITZ: Regardless of age, the pressures and uncertainties in our lives often make us long for someone who will help us overcome our fears—something that is difficult to achieve alone. "I am resting in the palm of God's hand" is a rather graphic image of what people are searching for. Actually, the idea of giving oneself over to a higher power is a central part of Islam and many other religions, as well as the Catholic faith.

Religious people, or those who live spiritually, feel themselves well off in a way that doesn't just have to do with money. At the center of their belief is the thought, "You are not alone; you are looked after." Every person who knows that a greater power is looking after his or her needs, feels rich, regardless of how great his or her income is. It is like having an all-inclusive life insurance policy. Frequently people only discover during a visit to a monastery or another spiritual institute how well off they really are. A monk who has taken the vow of poverty feels that he is rich.

Rapid progress often makes us wish that there could be a standstill. As our world is becoming ever more fast-paced, each of us needs a place of reflection and peace from time to time. You learn this in a monastery, whether you meditate for a few minutes each day or devote your entire life to contemplation. Living in a monastery for some time offers the chance to come to rest, to regard important questions of life, and to explore—to find inner equilibrium or simply focus on it all at once. I see it as a mental cleansing process which helped me to win back my creative strength and energy after my time in the monastery, and which has given me time for inner growth. You could call it a "flourishing of the soul."

ANSELM GRÜN: Like you, many managers need to withdraw to a monastery for a few days. There, they can structure their time according to their own rhythms, as it suits them, or take part in one of the spiritual leadership seminars which we offer in the abbey. In these seminars we want to communicate the Benedictine principles of management. This includes not only management methods but also paths to one's self, to stillness, and to the depths of one's own soul.

There are also some who want to stay, and these always include young men who knock on the monastery gate because they cannot come to terms with life in the world "outside." But that is an exception, and these men quickly understand that this is no real motive for entering the monastery. They would soon feel overburdened there, too. Most men who join us have successfully completed professional training or even worked in their professions. They enter the monastery primarily for spiritual reasons: they want to have time for meditation and prayer, for quiet and reading. And they would like to be supported by a community and continue to search for God and the secret of their own lives.

Yet many enter the monastery because they are searching for meaningful activity. They want to see the fruits of their work while maintaining a proper work-life balance. They have the impression that their work in the monastery is not only useful, but could also shape the world in a positive fashion. They don't need to give top priority to a boss's orders, but can think and plan with others, considering what the monastery might do for the world in the future. Of course, all this has to pay its way financially, but in a monastery you are not locked into a particular activity. There is room here for development of the individual's abilities, and many monks discover their artistic, literary, craft, or teaching abilities here. These two aspects—living a spiritual life and carrying out meaningful activity—are reason enough for these young men to join.

Large salaries are not an option for them here. Of course they have the guarantee of a certain living standard, which definitely turns out to be more modest than if they had stayed in their professions, but it is still enough to lead a good life. What is crucial is their sense of a spiritual longing in themselves which they cannot adequately live in their "old" lives. This is what leads them to search for a monastery where they can authentically live the search for God and the secret of humankind and Creation, while also contributing something to the well-being of humankind.

JOCHEN ZEITZ: Companies attract and keep employees primarily through their wages. However, a company must also give an employee identity, a sense of belonging and satisfaction through the work and company. It must offer the individual a rationale and the feeling of solidarity, which also helps to reduce uncertainty in difficult times. The community in a firm has a job similar to that of the family, clubs, or religious communities: it makes employees part of a team with an objective and purpose.

ANSELM GRÜN: I know many executive managers who pay lip service to the idea of employee solidarity, but encourage

29

separations because they are divided inside themselves. For this reason, developing a spirit of shared identity requires working on yourself: being at one with yourself and being ready to gather up everything within you when you go to meet others—not meeting them as a half-person who is only bringing your intellect to the encounter. When I go to meet others with everything that is in me, this sets up a flow between us. An outpouring of energy is transmitted between individuals when there is a feeling of shared identity, and they feel supported by the others. Therefore for me, one of the most important jobs of a manager is to develop a feeling for solidarity.

CHAPTER 3

CULTURE

WITH AN INTRODUCTION BY
JOCHEN ZEITZ

As individuals and cultural groups, we are seemingly separate from each other, and yet we are connected by a common past. An island may appear as a separate land mass, but if you could divert the water around it, you would discover that the island is the peak of an underwater mountain range. It is the same with culture, too: we human beings appear to be divided from each other as if by oceans—and yet we are firmly connected through a common history, a common geography, a common memory, and a common social climate. No one is an island.

Carl Jung taught us that we human beings have a shared memory, which could be called the social memory. He explains that we are closely tied to each other in our subconscious; and that everywhere in the world, regardless of the cultural environment to which we belong, we have the same—ancient—dreams and basic associations, such as the universal dream of flying, as if one and the same author had written a script for all our dreams and nightmares.[1]

According to Jung, shared memory and its subsidiary, the complete cultural memory, are factors that constantly influence human perception, both positively and negatively. An unbalanced culture

31

can have just as much (or even more) influence on the individual as a functioning or nonfunctioning basic culture. Therefore it is important to consider the kind of culture from which an individual's current experiences arise. This holds as true for the manager and the monk in their respectively formed communities.

Cultural memories and traditions can seem fixed, delaying the cultural change of a nation or a company. Most social movements only develop slowly and gain dynamic force bit by bit, having to struggle in the beginning with fierce resistance in some parts. When managers gain influence or step up into leadership positions, they ought to ask themselves which style of culture best suits the company they are joining. They must consider: How does the climate have to change? How can I build up the desired interaction and maintain it? Do we need a permanent culture or one that constantly adapts? Which elements of the collective memory can be effectively recognized, what must be brought in, and what must be discarded? How do we ensure that cultural identity and transformation really take hold and are more than superficial window dressing? And finally, a manager must confront the question: How can we honor ethnic, cultural, and personal diversity and apply them to our advantage? I am convinced that bosses who don't ask themselves these questions and don't learn from them are condemned to long-term defeat.

PUMA'S CULTURE

Soon after joining PUMA, I discovered that a company's culture is a matter of great significance. In the course of many years I was able to observe and influence the way groups worked together. The goal was always to create a proper environment for our efforts for balance and growth.

Initially, we needed to set our future course in practical terms, and so English was decided on as our first language, in spite of our German origins. That was not an obvious step to take when you consider that the majority of my colleagues spoke no English, or hardly any, when I joined the company in 1990. On another occasion, a decision had to be reached as to whether we ought to attempt (like so many other German companies at the time) to oversee marketing, product development, and sales in North America entirely from Europe. The alternative was to work on site in North America, Asia, and elsewhere to merge the best elements of international business practice into a new culture.

One of the most important questions that needed consideration and involved motivating our employees—mostly against their own convictions—was the market positioning of our brand and company. We decided to transform ourselves from a sporting goods manufacturer to a sport lifestyle provider, to generate a new market for ourselves and for the consumer. But there were a number of employees who did not want to let go of the old model. When we showed a skateboarder in our branded video, for example, to emphasize the new positioning as a sports lifestyle brand, I received criticism and disapproval from many sides. This change was thought to be inappropriate for a company which until then had oriented itself exclusively to performance and sport. But once the commotion dies down and people can see and feel the success of the new model, then a company culture can grow and flourish—provided that you foster creativity and allow its effects to unfold throughout the company, rather than suddenly changing your strategy. Since that time, our business has reached far beyond offering just functional sport textiles and shoes. The fashion and lifestyle aspect for PUMA, expressed through the design and styling of our clothing, shoes, and accessories, is just as important.

At times, when our company and its brand recorded nothing but setbacks, and few employees really wanted to go in new directions, we considered transferring PUMA to another city or even another country. We felt then as if failure and negative thinking were clinging to the walls of our buildings. Quite a few people at PUMA favored tearing down all bridges to the past before assembling a new, successful team. Yet we kept Herzogenaurach as our corporate headquarters while simultaneously broadening our global presence and enlarging our virtual and cosmopolitan presences. Before everything else, we aimed to have a foothold in the United States, where the PUMA brand played hardly any role at that time. In 1997 I therefore decided to guide the firm's development myself from Boston for five years in order to become better acquainted with the inspiring "American way of life," and to integrate it into our company culture. (A number of employees were fearful at the time that the company head office would also be relocated to the United States.) Our marketing and an important part of our product development were administered out of Boston. We also established an Asian regional office in Hong Kong for product procurement, and to be one step closer to the emerging Asian markets.

Initially, I had to travel back and forth constantly between different continents and cultures, a wanderer between worlds. I felt as if I were a preacher as I tried to bring together the different mentalities and cultures characterizing PUMA (which were supposed to lead to a better future) and attempted to interpret between them. The various parties hardly talked to each other, or just didn't understand each other. From this situation, a shared, interconnected and unique PUMA culture developed little by little—certainly not overnight. This culture helped us to think and act globally. Eventually it was effective in overcoming the past, with its failures and doubts about newness, without giving up our heritage or history.

Last but not least, we had to make overall psychological decisions, because there are several different cultural levels in a company, as Edgar Schein at MIT's Sloan School of Management has described so well. According to Schein, at the uppermost cultural level of a company is its appearance or "look."[2] This includes its

34

buildings, furniture, and clothing. Its overt identity features, such as image, mission statement, and company marketing, follow on the next level. Finally there is the essence of the company, the heart, its deeper cultural identity. This cannot be determined either by a single person or by a sort of company "culture police": it can only develop positively and successfully when a critical mass of individuals supports this company spirit and takes responsibility for seeing that its shared values are respected. This is why it was so important for me to involve many different groups and employees in the creation of our vision. Only when employees feel involved in the development of the company will they contribute to identify with it, investing themselves and their energy to promote the company in a positive way.

I personally felt that PUMA needed to develop a positive, creative, entrepreneurially driven, open, and sincere culture. Yet it was just as important for me that others on my team be in agreement with this vision and want to make it a reality. No one is an island. A vision can be created by a single individual at the beginning, but a culture has to be shaped by many people. And an open and creative culture doesn't just affect many people; it must be carried by almost all of them.

In no way do I want to leave the impression that we are the perfect company. On the contrary: we still have a fair way to go to become a top-ranking firm. Over the years I have also made mistakes, from which I tried to learn as much as I could. Some of these mistakes crept in because I was excessively driven: sometimes I tried to achieve too much too soon, and took on too much at once. Sometimes, for example, I was busy with my BlackBerry and computer—to the disappointment of some people—during colleagues' presentations. Or I took too little time to talk with employees in person. Such shortcuts are often the result of speeding things up, and I had to learn to put on the brakes and move ahead more slowly.

A GOOD LEADER ALSO INSPIRES

One of the most important aspects of a creative company culture concerns the way in which it is implemented. Instead of applying the old John Wayne model ("Follow me, men!"), creative cultures are open and create opportunities for everyone to be a leading figure and blaze a trail by good example. In creative cultures, different backgrounds and styles are welcome. Good executive managers working in an evolving cultural framework can awaken those qualities which remain dormant in others, and can inspire employees.

Just as John Wayne was a role model for me in my childhood, there are other heroes today who inspire me, such as the author and environmental activist Paul Hawken, who wrote *Blessed Unrest* and *Natural Capitalism,* among other books. Or Auret van Heerden, who was involved as a student in the South African anti-apartheid movement, and is head of the Fair Labor Association today. Or Gregory David Roberts, a visionary who overcame many obstacles in his early life and wrote one of my favorite books, *Shantaram.* He helped me to develop our PUMAVision.

Regarding culture, in my opinion, the most important leadership goals include integration, an open exchange of ideas, building confidence, and striving for greater quality. A leadership culture also has to be fun, and it must promote meaningfulness and innovation, regardless of how close to the wind you may sail sometimes. Here as well, I still have things to learn about the right rhythm. Sometimes I surprise myself even today by keeping my eyes fixed on the next dark cloud on the horizon, instead of taking shore leave at the right time and urging my team to enjoy shared successes before we head back to sea.

If we abbreviate the word *culture,* we get the restrictive word *cult.* And all shortcuts which we take in building up a complete, extensive, and developing culture lead to rigid cult behavior. Companies that follow a cult instead of a culture petrify into tired bureaucracies; they become "old men's clubs." They fare badly in comparison to companies whose structures are organic and always in flux. This is why a dynamic, future-oriented culture makes the difference between a living business spirit and dead, dull thinking.

PUMA had to be changed in a rational fashion from a conservative, traditional worldview centered on Germany to an open, cosmopolitan focus with a global consciousness. Our task is never finished: we are still developing, and our surroundings are constantly changing. Today we have to prove our sensitivity to the rapid change of economic and ecological conditions and times, without giving up our standards and our multicultural structure in the process.

Finally, maintaining a holistic and animated, dynamic culture is an important job of a manager, in addition to supporting and stimulating others with new ideas. Those are not easy tasks in view of the ethnic, cultural, and personal diversity that characterize a worldwide, growing team.

Managers inspire when they lead by example and involve others in an invigorating atmosphere, however difficult the economic situation and their own business may be. When I took on a job with the then unfortunate PUMA company, I was mostly laughed at and inundated with critical questions and skepticism. I had just turned twenty-seven years of age. Added to that was the fact that I had broken with my own family's tradition in which medicine—either as research or in clinical practice—was the profession of choice. I felt myself strengthened in my own determination, and it motivates me when others say, "That won't work!"

DIALOGUE: MANAGER AND MONK

ANSELM GRÜN: If we look at our culture, religions have influenced societies continuously up to our own time. Today, on the contrary, one has the impression that the economy is shaping cities more and more. In earlier times the Church was in the center of a city, and gave it its own character. Today cities distinguish themselves with corporate skyscrapers. But the interaction of people, the way they think and feel, how they manage the milestones of their lives such as birth, marriage, and death: all that continues to be marked by religion. It will be important for business and religion to go hand in hand.

The values that religion embodies and the rituals it offers for reaching peace and reflecting on the deeper meaning of life ought to be heeded by the people who have responsibility in companies. Such people need to listen to God and the quiet impulse of their own souls in order to situate their work within a broader horizon; in addition, they need to contextualize work through religion. If they define themselves only through work and success, they will become grim. Then work will not be a blessing for them, their employees, or the people to whom the company sells its product. Action in the business world really needs its own laws. Religion ought not to have the right to stipulate management methods in detail; if it did, it would take on totalitarian traits. But the economy ought not to become totalitarian, either, or everything in our lives would be determined solely by financial factors. This would take the breath of life away from humankind and society.

Religion keeps open the inquiry about God in a closed society. That is beneficial for humankind, because when we keeps ourselves open to God, we cannot be manipulated by the economy. The open heaven over our Earth allows us to live well here. It opens up a space of freedom and breadth for us. When everything is merely governed according to an economic point of view, life becomes increasingly narrow and sad.

JOCHEN ZEITZ: If you look back at history, you realize that business and religion have developed and grown in parallel ways, always with a strong interplay. The early monasteries, which also functioned as companies, demonstrated that the world of religion and the world of business were often dependent on each other. While the advice of religious spokespeople is still sought everywhere (as it always has been), including in the public domain, universities and even religious colleges—principally in the Anglo-Saxon world—are increasingly appointing experienced business celebrities to their advisory committees and boards of directors.

If you look at early cultures such as ancient Greece, you see that it was quite customary to seek the advice or blessing of the gods and bring in the priests before building a new house, setting off on a trip, or beginning a new business undertaking. (I still encounter this personally today, by the way, in my travels—particularly in Asia.) Moreover, the old temples and cathedrals could only have been built with the support and financing of patrons, governments, carpenters, and others. So business acumen was of course also required for all ventures of this kind.

Various religions indicate that there is no Yin without Yang, no light without darkness, no heaven without hell, and in my view this opposition of pairs also applies to the spiritual and material worlds. One cannot help Man to appreciate transcendent things without practical rudiments. But practical elements have little purpose or context if they lack a spiritual context.

ANSELM GRÜN: For me, there are different points of connection between religion and business. The exterior one, which you referred to—seeking the blessing of the gods or the priests before building a new house, or before

39

planning a business—is still practiced today. Sometimes I am invited to consecrate a dental practice or a bookstore or the new office of a firm. Usually it is mid-sized companies that explicitly request God's blessing for their work. They have the feeling that their own actions do not determine everything, and that God's blessing has an important role. They are not soliciting God's blessing in order to do better business, but rather to bring protection for the people who work at the place, and to allow clients who come to the dentist, for example, to experience healing and encouragement within a blessed space in the practice. Business owners who want to begin their enterprises with God's blessing are convinced that relations between their employees don't depend entirely on the boss's personality but are also shaped by God's benediction. This often relaxes the atmosphere in a business.

The other point of connection between religion and business is religion's criticism of certain styles of management. The prophets in Israel had the duty of criticizing the behavior of the powerful. The prophet Amos is a primary example: he constantly addressed the consciences of the rich and those in power, telling them that they were oppressing the poor and demanding unjust taxes. Amos prophesied that because of this, their actions would not be blessed: "Because you trample on the poor and take from them levies of grain, you have built houses of hewn stone, but you shall not live in them; you have planted pleasant vineyards, but you shall not drink their wine" (Amos 5:11).

Religion cannot dictate to the economy how it ought to proceed, for it often doesn't know the laws of economics. But religion does have a duty to denounce unfair and antisocial consequences of trade and commerce, and to lay down criteria which ought to be considered in management. Religions have always been advocates for people, yet even religion can lead to the oppression of people when it is misused. The Bible describes how Jesus chastised the Pharisees for saddling other people with burdens instead of freeing them from oppression. This phenomenon can be found in all religions, and thus management has a duty to be critical of entrenched religious structures.

JOCHEN ZEITZ: Both business and religion need that well-intentioned yet critical gaze from the other party. Managers and monks would do well to make the strengths of the other their own. Father Anselm, you and your abbey need the approach of a manager to a certain extent: you must know what is functioning well from an economic point of view, who is suitable for a certain job or position, and how the monastery is represented publicly, in order to make it attractive and relevant. This includes the seminar programs, rental of space, and so on. All these are necessary managerial skills which I personally took note of in your monastery. Monks must know their abbot as a person of integrity who is qualified to consider possibilities and make the right decision. As you always emphasize, Father Anselm, a Benedictine monastery has to be able to finance itself. In order to fulfill its primary religious duties, you must manage your monastery successfully, and for this you must develop a manager's skills, including a clear mission and vision.

Seen from the purely commercial standpoint of a manager, it would be possible, in my view, for an abbot or cellarer and a manager to trade places. Of course there are challenges, including credible communication and representation of each one's mission and vision,

41

and adapting to the size, the sequence of events, and the atmosphere of the circumstances in each place. Then there is the obligation to account for one's actions to the appropriate participants: seekers, suppliers, cardinals, committees, customers, shareholders, converts, unions, and many more, who speak different languages and pursue their own agendas.

ANSELM GRÜN: I would also believe myself to be capable of running a worldly company, but I observe that everything that goes beyond a mid-sized enterprise would present considerable problems for me. That is definitely connected with the kind of experiences I have had in the monastery. With three hundred employees, we are a mid-sized company. Leading a large firm like PUMA would not only be difficult for me, but the continuous moving around is not my thing. Of course, I do travel quite a bit to give my lectures, yet my work in administration is rooted to the soil and has defined limits. As a monastery we are not under as much pressure as a "worldly" company that asserts itself in the world market and must act with greater flexibility than a monastery.

Yet when I experienced the conference at PUMA concerning implementation of the sustainability concept, I sensed that I also had a desire to set standards in a company which could change the whole business climate. That is also the appeal of a large enterprise: not that it makes the greatest possible profit, but that it shapes the world, helps to set the tone, and brings new ideas into the world.

Another common feature of the leadership positions in our two companies is loneliness. Even the abbot and the cellarer belong to the community of the monastery, but of course the abbot experiences a certain loneliness in his position. He must keep many personal problems to himself which his fellow Brothers confide to him. He cannot justify his behavior toward certain of his fellow Brothers to everyone, because he must protect their confidentiality. The abbot shares this loneliness with the head of a company. Monastic as well as secular executives need many skills. . . .

JOCHEN ZEITZ: And both must be role models, and remain capable of stopping themselves and their colleagues from becoming fixed in old patterns of thinking and acting. If you are aiming at a new way of doing things, then every employee and every manager must find his own recipe for preserving an open attitude and being able to regard his company and his own life with the eyes of another person, observing as if from outside.

I can only speak for myself: deep in my heart, I am eager to learn, and I am adventure-loving by nature. Because I travel a lot and have lived and studied in many different countries, I can say that speaking different languages and exploring other cultures help me to better understand cultural diversity and really hold it in high esteem. I have learned that you have to hear both sides of a story, because this very valuable approach is a necessary precondition for making better decisions and being a better manager. To me, diversity is a source of energy and creativity.

I often seek advice from a consultant or supervisor who helps me to improve my comprehension of the fields of psychology and theology, which I regard as fundamental prerequisites for the broadening of my personal awareness. In addition to this, my own foundation, which is supported by ambassadors and experts with different backgrounds and

43

origins, gives me new perspectives on an ongoing basis, and not only in the area of ecological sustainability. Travel, listening, getting advice: all this, together with an adventure-loving curiosity, helps me to maintain an open attitude in my professional career as well as my life as a whole.

ANSELM GRÜN: Of course there is also cultural inertia in monasteries. I have visited other monasteries to advise them in a business capacity, and I have sometimes been shocked to see how ingrained many things were. Certainly everyone worked hard, but the organization was highly inefficient. They managed as they always had before, and then lamented that their funds were insufficient, rather than going in new directions.

I hold lectures in other countries and enjoy inquiring into other mind-sets. I am pleased that my thoughts are also understood in South America and Asia, but I don't overcome cultural inertia by immersion in foreign cultures. The length of my visits in a given place are much too short for that. For me reading is of first importance, and reflecting. I also try to listen to the people whom I accompany or who ask me questions at the lectures. Then when I travel home after the lecture, I try to put myself into these people's shoes: what do they need? And how can we, as monks, answer their questions? That keeps my pastoral work alive.

But I also ask myself how we can answer people's questions with our type of management. What should we produce? What do people expect of us? Where could we create alternatives to the increasingly bureaucratic ways of management, which are often essentially shaped by fear? What is our contribution to sustainability, to a different management culture, to a form of managing which has a future? Listening to people, talking with them, and listening to my own heart keep me alive and protect me from growing rigid in my actions. Yet I always need space and quiet for this, in order to listen in stillness to what my heart wants to say.

JOCHEN ZEITZ: You say that our management is determined by fear. Fear is a truly important theme today; many people are afraid of losing their jobs, for example. Yet there is no long-term guarantee in life (until death), and therefore we must be prepared and live with uncertainty in many areas of our existence.

When a major company is caught up in financial difficulties, it is understandably hard to persuade some employees (who fear the loss of their positions) that it is necessary to alter our course and bring in extensive changes. A manager can be fighting a losing battle when he wants to restructure or save a business by making fundamental decisions. In challenging situations like these, I have found that you have only a few allies, because sluggishness, fear, and uncertainty make people regard change skeptically and unwillingly at first.

It was astonishing to me to see that at the beginning of the 1990s—even after years of losses—"business as usual" was still a given part of the basic attitude at PUMA. At the time, it took an enormous effort to bring about rapid change and implement the necessary change consistently.

After the various radical business upheavals that I have lived through, I recommend patience and understanding to anyone who wants to change the status quo at a company. Real cultural change happens slowly, and for this reason change needs to be a constant presence if it is to have lasting effects. You have to understand that there will be resistance to change at the beginning, and that it will dissolve into thin air once there is clear success. Change is possible in a large corporation if you decide to go forward and then bring about changes little by little, while winning over allies one after the other. However long the journey, it begins with the first step. Tenacity and patience together are a successful combination.

ANSELM GRÜN: For us it is less a matter of anxiety about jobs impeding restructuring as the feeling, "It has always been that way. That is just what we need." When we confronted the question of whether or not to build our own laundry facility, I had clearly reckoned that it would not be worthwhile. But I came up against great resistance: it was unimaginable for many of the older monks to entrust their dirty laundry to an outside washing facility. When I added it all up for them, however, they were convinced. I tried to listen to the arguments of the older brothers, and in this way we found a course of action that has satisfied everyone so far. Something similar happened in the combining of kitchens for the boarding school and monastery, and with many other restructurings. It is important to take notice of opposition and listen to it, but there is no point in yielding to every expression of resistance. It is important instead to recognize what message is being communicated: often those in opposition are merely stalling, and fail to identify any alternatives. Then you cannot give in. Sometimes opposition is an expression of anxiety. I have to take such cases seriously and try to respond and refute them. I have also observed that this takes patience, and I must be careful not to judge. My first reaction was often to say to myself: this or that person is narrow-minded, just blocking everything; he is intransigent. But it is important to get involved with every person so that I can bring everybody

46

along in the same boat. When some individuals don't want to come along, that is their decision which I must respect. In a firm, such an employee might leave the company at this point. In a monastery you must see to it that in the future he is employed where he can make a contribution with his abilities, instead of being obstructive.

CHAPTER 4

VALUES

WITH AN INTRODUCTION BY
ANSELM GRÜN

When companies have invited me to speak over the past few years, they have increasingly requested the topics "Leadership with Values" or "Values and Managing." Many businesspeople in positions of responsibility sense that we cannot manage permanently without values. When companies ignore values, they become worthless in the long term, because those who disregard values are treating humankind and themselves with disdain. An atmosphere of despising oneself and others will quickly make a firm worthless. Its capital vanishes. Staff who are treated with disdain and who despise themselves will lose all feeling of solidarity. This situation can cause a company to collapse.

Many firms today try to support the cause of values to help them orient themselves. For example, one German firm has dressed itself up with the formula "Creating Value by Valuing Highly." In the meantime, business management analyses show that firms that orient themselves around values are more successful in the long term than those which are only interested in making money quickly. When we talk about values, however, we should promote them rather than simply moralizing, for if we only arouse pangs of conscience in people, they will not be interested in values. Values make life valuable, and give a company enduring self-worth.

Values are also related to dignity: they protect the dignity of the individual. The person who sees herself as having importance doesn't feel it is necessary to devalue others. She can be pleased about the value of others, and recognize and support it. The person who regards himself as worthless, however, has to disparage others constantly in order to tolerate himself.

The Latin word for value, *virtus*, means "strength, a source of strength." Values are sources from which we take strength. The English word *value* comes from the Latin word *valere*, meaning "to be healthy" or "to be strong." By extension, then, values keep us and our interactions healthy, and boost our work together.

Twenty-five hundred years ago, the Greek philosophers, headed by Plato, described four fundamental human values: justice (or righteousness), courage, moderation, and practical intelligence. The Christian tradition took these from the Greek philosophers and called them the "cardinal virtues." They added three further values: faith, hope, and love. These values are also connected with the fundamental essence of humanity independently of Western culture. They preserve the dignity of people in all religions and cultures, even though they have different names in diverse human languages—and they still have validity today.

JUSTICE, COURAGE, MODERATION, AND PRACTICAL INTELLIGENCE

Justice (or righteousness) is the first named of these basic human values. For Plato, justice means first of all being fair to oneself and one's character, and honoring one's body, soul, and spirit in a suitable way. The individual who is fair to himself doesn't allow himself to be corrupted, but goes on his way in an upright and honest manner. He will also comfort others, and this gives justice a social component: being fair to other people. The Romans had an expression for this: *suum cuique*—giving each his own. This principle leads to justice between individuals, including the fair division of goods, just distribution of opportunities, fair educational opportunities, and fair wages.

Jesus says that those people who hunger and thirst after righteousness are blessed. He knows that we will not achieve absolute righteousness here on Earth, yet he maintains that we must always endeavor to create just structures and opportunities, both in companies and in the entire world. It says in the Bible, "He who sows righteousness will harvest peace." Without righteousness there is no peace—in a firm, a family, or the world. When a company is governed by unjust structures, much energy is lost because people exhaust themselves and fight instead of putting their energy into their work. When everything is organized fairly and properly, this energy is freed up for planning and carrying out activities. In unjust relationships there are constant trench wars between rival groups and within the hierarchy. Justice, then, is a real source of strength for individuals and for a company.

In a company that is active worldwide, however, justice should be applied at more than just one location. A firm like PUMA must see to it that it deals fairly with its individual operating units in different countries. What the company does must be right for all people in all parts of the world. Firms that have incorporated fair company structures aren't merely exporting goods: they are exporting values as well. Through a fair system of payment and fair treatment of employees they create a climate that spreads out into and influences society.

The second value Plato talks about is *courage*. This means the courage to stand up for my own convictions and fight for them, even when I may be exhausted or wounded for doing this. The brave person doesn't bend. He remains clearly by himself. Bravery

51

isn't stubbornness; it is a readiness to take responsibility for myself and what I represent before others, even if I will be rejected, criticized, or even fought on account of this. Today, we would describe this kind of bravery as having the courage of one's convictions.

Many people today take their cue from the opinion of the majority. Finding no value in themselves, they become dependent on the validation of others' approval, and become yes-men who hide themselves in the crowd. Bravery also denotes the courage to stand by uncomfortable decisions when you are convinced of their soundness. The brave person doesn't communicate her decisions anonymously; she has the courage to look others in the face and stand behind her own opinion.

Plato's third value is the "right measure," or *moderation*. Saint Benedict calls this "wise moderation," and for him this is the "mother of all virtues." Moderation is not mediocrity, but rather the art of handling oneself, others, and nature in a moderate way. Today, we would call this ancient virtue *sustainability*. Benedict recognizes three Latin words for measure: *mensura, temperare,* and *discretio. Mensura* means the right measure in terms of my own self-assessment. Many people become ill today because they place immoderate demands on themselves: they think they must always be successful, always perfect, always in a good mood, always cool, always seeing everything positively. The "right measure" means that I assess my weaknesses and my strengths correctly.

The second word for measure, *temperare*, is derived from the Latin word *tempus*—time. This type of moderation is principally concerned with duration. Someone who is constantly working against his own inner rhythm is very quickly exhausted. Yet as Jung maintains, the person who follows his own rhythm at work is capable of working more. Reading, for example, can be done according to the nature of this activity; it has its own rhythm. A person who gets into that rhythm will be able to work more. Rituals are an important means of finding one's own inner rhythm. They give me the feeling that I am living myself, instead of being lived from outside. Rituals create a sacred time: a time belonging to myself which no other person can control. We need such inviolable times in order to be intact, to be completely in ourselves. Rituals close one door and open another, but many people don't close the door to work in the evenings, and so they don't really come home. They are unresponsive, with their thoughts still focused on the workday. The wife of a university director once said to her husband, "When we are sitting in the living room, I want to talk with you." Her husband often doesn't "close the door" on the university; everything that occupies him there is still on his mind, getting in the way of communication with his wife. For the person who never closes the door on work, the door of his home doesn't really open. He is absent, though he is there. You might say he is always standing in the hallway.

The third term for moderation, *discretio*, means the gift of differentiation. I myself need a good sense for distinguishing individuals in my work: I shouldn't think of everyone as being the same, because I must empathize with each individual and imagine what he or she needs and what his or her measure is. When I know these things about others, I can assess people better and employ them properly. Then they can become a blessing for a company. In this way I won't demand too much of individuals, but will handle their resources in a sustainable way.

The fourth virtue, according to Plato, is *practical intelligence*. This is the ability to make the right decision for the moment, considering what is possible and desirable in the concrete circumstances of the world economy and the situation in a company. Practical intelligence dismisses overly ambitious ideals; it is the ability to link great ideas with daily reality. Thomas Aquinas, one of the most important Church teachers and a medieval philosopher, maintains that this wisdom (*prudentia* in Latin) comes from foresight (in Latin, *providentia*). Wisdom requires vision and a broader horizon. Only when I have a vision, when I look past the moment, can I decide correctly now, in this instant. The intelligent person has a sense for people and sees in advance how an individual will behave. An intelligent individual is always a seer—someone who looks more deeply, who is careful. She doesn't simply act, but first looks at precisely what she is doing and where that will lead.

FAITH, HOPE, AND LOVE

Aside from these four basic values of the Greek philosophers, the Christian tradition preached three further values: faith, hope, and love.

Faith is not only a matter of believing in God, but also of belief in human beings. The person who believes in God must also believe in the people God created. Faith in God gives us confidence that what we do will be a blessing for this world. It releases us from constant spiritual vacillation about whether we are doing everything properly, or what others might think about us. We trust that God will make our decisions and the things we have undertaken into a blessing for the company and for human beings as well; but it is God who determines this in the last resort—not our intelligence or our strength. Faith gives us a foundation in God that frees us from the judgments of other people. My experience shows that managers who believe in God are more relaxed. They feel themselves supported by a higher power.

Saint Benedict demands that we monks see Christ in every brother and sister, so we are supposed to have faith in the good core of each human being. That does not mean that we go around with rose-colored glasses and believe that all people are only good, but we refuse to be fixated on an individual's often negative facade. Faith means looking to the very foundation of the other person, and recognizing the longing for goodness there. Because I believe in the good in another person, I can also awaken this quality.

Today many companies and many parts of society speak in a cold, hard, antihuman, condemnatory, and judgmental language. The language of faith is a comforting language that comes from the heart and names the good in people. The way in which I speak to and about other human beings reveals whether I believe in them or am nonbelieving in the final analysis. Many executives who want to continuously motivate their employees fail to believe in them, in their good essence. Faith awakes the good in employees. It is an active power which achieves something in a human being: if I believe in someone, I enable him to believe in himself, too.

Faith must become audible and palpable in the way in which we speak with and to our employees. We are building a house with language. The question, then, is whether we are building a house of faith or one without faith; a house that is cold inside, which everyone would prefer to leave again as quickly as possible; or a house in which people warm themselves, where they enjoy spending time with each other and tackling their work.

The second Christian value is *hope*. Dante thought that life without hope would become hell. No one can lead a company or a corporate group without having hope. Hope is something different from expectation, because the expectation I have for a person or a company can be disappointed. Hoping, on the other hand, means: "I am hoping for you and about you." Hope can never be disappointed, because I will not give up the hope that another person will be able to change himself.

The apostle Paul says that we hope for something that we cannot see. I am hoping, on behalf of an employee, for something that is still invisible in him. I will not give him up. I believe him capable of developing himself. Ernst Bloch, the philosopher of hope, asserts that the only things that are valuable are those which are interwoven with hope and communicated by hope. A good architect doesn't merely build houses—he builds hope: hope for security, for a home and safety, for beauty. A company, then, is only valuable in the long term when it spreads hope through its treatment of its employees and customers, and with its products. In relations with customers, my personality can communicate the hope that it is worthwhile to live, and that we can make life more worth living. And where my products are concerned, I should always ask myself whether they transmit hope to the purchasers that their lives will be more valuable, more beautiful, more humane, and more satisfying.

The last value—*love*—may sound much too pious for many people. In Greek philosophy and also in the Bible, love is not so much a commandment as a source from which we can create, and a power that changes our lives. A well of goodwill and love is bubbling in everyone. In the First Letter of John in the New Testament, you can read that God is love. And whoever is within love is also within God. Through love, then, we participate in God.

Love is a source of strength. When, for example, I go to a meeting with the feeling that I will now have to argue with some peculiar people, I will certainly have a headache afterwards. But when I go there with basic goodwill, a different energy comes into being, and afterward I often feel inwardly refreshed. In psychology one speaks of "energy robbers" and "energy boosters." A meeting where everyone fights with everyone else robs me of all energy. However, when I go into a conference with goodwill and even with love, I come out refreshed afterwards, in spite of two hours of work, because I have received energy. In the last analysis, I can only fill employees with enthusiasm for the goals I set if I love them. If they sense that I despise them, that I don't care about them, they will not let themselves be motivated. Or to put this in Jesus's words: "His sheep follow him because they know his voice. They will not follow a stranger, but they will run from him because they do not know the voice of strangers" (John 10:4–5). The person who loves his employees knows them, and they know him. When someone despises them, they flee from him and are wary of him. They take refuge in working according to instructions, but they will not follow him in the direction which he sets, even if he leads the way himself.

Values make life worthwhile and give lasting worth to an enterprise. It is an important duty for administrators not only to be a living example of values, but to communicate them in a way that makes employees want to emulate them. When you "limp along" with a bad conscience behind values, you will not foster a climate of eagerness or enthusiasm; instead you will overstrain the company with moralizing demands, which will lead to mutual judgments and the suspicion that others are only giving lip service to values without actually living them. It is our task to promote values in a way that awakens our employees' appetite for life and pleasure in working together.

DIALOGUE: MANAGER AND MONK

JOCHEN ZEITZ: The Bible communicates these values, but at first glance the Bible seems to have no influence on companies today. In our multicultural world, many employees have completely different religious backgrounds, while others are atheists, agnostics, or searchers after meaning. But in my opinion, the influence of the Bible is subconsciously present everywhere, like the air that we breathe. Because of the way many of us were brought up and think, some of the contents of the Bible affect and guide the way we deal with other people and nature.

For many of us, given our education and cultural development in a Christian society, the Bible (in the form of the Ten Commandments and other teachings) determines many basic norms of human coexistence in our subconscious minds. These doctrines go beyond a religious horizon; they extend to all spheres of society, even the business world.

Christian businesses do exist where employees pray together during breaks, and the company strives for an almost priestly demeanor in the workplace. I experienced this myself at a company in Korea where the employees had to march in the morning and pray during the day. However, that appeared to be more a facade than truly lived Christianity. Most businesses are secular in their orientation, and in many of them a mentality of "survival of the fittest" replaces the commandment to "love they neighbor." In my view, a manager's job is to exercise authority with the greatest possible understanding and circumspection, so that he can look after balance and inspiration in the workplace—whether he personally draws on the teachings of the Bible, the Torah, the Tao, the Koran, or other sacred and wise books.

ANSELM GRÜN: I am also acquainted with Christian companies that, although upholding the Bible, do not use its spirit to shape their conduct. Instead, they use the Bible to put themselves above others in their executive behavior. They use the Bible to justify their conduct instead of letting it call their actions into question. I believe that my duty is a matter of allowing myself to be illuminated anew by the words of Jesus, again and again. His words are concerned first and foremost with how I handle other people: whether I help them and give them the courage to believe in their own strengths, whether I myself show confidence in them, or condemn them. The Bible to me is an ongoing challenge to let myself be stamped with the spirit of Jesus.

The Bible is a book that I read again and again, and after reading it, I try to model my thoughts and deeds on it. But I cannot use it as a weapon and order others to model themselves on it in the same way. That would be counterproductive. Instead, I want to try to make the spirit of the Bible real for my employees and customers—through my own person and my dealings with other people and with Creation. But as monks we don't go peddling the Bible; it is more a matter of expressing its spirit, which is stamped on us.

JOCHEN ZEITZ: Managers today must actively follow a clearly defined chain of values in their work, whether or not this is based on religious conviction. When they are hiring employees, personnel managers today assign increasing importance to social intelligence as well as overall competence. A manager's ability to manage over and above ethical, cultural, and gender boundaries; and to show empathy while simultaneously "rallying the troops" is more important than ever before. Managers must convince employees of the company's vision, and support and encourage them in their striving for personal success.

On the subject of "rallying the troops": at PUMA we have banned every reference to and use of martial vocabulary and symbols of warfare. I always found it extremely disconcerting when one of our competitors would talk about the "battle for the soccer market," for example. We forbade this years ago, so this vocabulary really has no business here now.

Honesty seems to be a very valuable commodity these days. In the first decade of this new millennium, the truth was constantly and repeatedly denied, whether consciously or unconsciously—not only in the business world but also in sport, politics, and society as a whole. That is one reason why it was so important at PUMA to emphasize honesty as one of our four primary key values, and also to remedy or minimize our own deficit in this respect.

Furthermore, you can hardly overestimate the value of transparency. We work privately toward transparency in the areas of ecological and social sustainability. In light of this effort, all of us at PUMA were pleased when our sustainability report was recently singled out as "remarkable" by the Global Compact, an initiative of the United Nations, and our Environmental Profit & Loss Account was recognized by *The Guardian* as a major innovation and PUMA as the first to evaluate and monetize natural capital and a business's impact on the environment across the entire supply chain.

ANSELM GRÜN: What you call honesty and transparency, Mr. Zeitz, I like to call truthfulness, and I also feel that this virtue is particularly important today for good and rewarding coexistence in business. Honesty relates more to external behavior: I conduct myself so that I show honor to others and protect my own honor by doing this. Truthfulness means, in the first instance, the behavior of a human being toward him- or herself. The person is truthful who is in agreement with her inner being. Whoever is truthful in himself also tells the truth, and his entire conduct expresses the fact that you can rely on him, that he means what he says and how he acts. Truthfulness is the condition that makes our incarnation as human beings successful. It is the virtue that makes us wholly ourselves and wholly authentic.

Truthfulness is also needed for a sound community. That is true for a company just as much as for society. Community is destroyed by lies. Over time a firm can only exist when it faces up to the truth, when it tries to live inwardly what it represents to the outer world. Such truthfulness gives rise to a feeling of dependability. Employees feel they can depend on the executive, and customers can depend on the company and its products. Dependability is more important to the customer than a short-lived price advantage.

Today, many people long for individuals and businesses on whom they can depend. When we say "you can rely on this person," we mean that we can trust him. He is reliable, honest, trustworthy. This gives us a feeling of security. We don't need to verify everything; we can count on his work and his word. The truthful individual is always a dependable person as well. And a firm that takes up the cause of truthfulness and tries to live it will radiate dependability for its customers. In this way the company gives them a feeling of security.

JOCHEN ZEITZ: In addition to the values you have cited, which stem from Christian and Greek tradition, there is a concept which has nothing in common with the value ethic yet is a solid component of our linguistic usage: money as value.

Today's economic model essentially sets up a standard for measuring all commercial activity. Briefly stated, this model reaches the conclusion that money = value. A global currency valuation system has been created which measures everything by monetary criteria. It is possible to incorporate traditional values within this system, but the ultimate goal is to achieve shareholder value through increased profit—in other words, monetary value for the shareholders.

In the beginning, money and the price system were helpful for society, for they offered a simple means of measuring the relative value of material goods. But in our modern world, with billions of currency units that can be transferred electronically in seconds, I question whether we can assess the extent and value of money at all anymore. The definition of money is no longer static (if indeed it ever was), and its value is no longer dependent on culture,

61

the market, or the decade in which we live. Instead, it depends more on what (if anything) it is secured against, in this debt-plagued global economy.

ANSELM GRÜN: The problem of today's monetary economy, however, is that money is becoming more dependent all the time on economic management. Previously, a company was thought to need profit in order to reinvest it, thus facilitating growth or a good outlook. Today, many banks speculate in the money market independently of their business transactions, but their speculations can drive entire national economies into ruin or force certain markets in a direction that eventually benefits nobody except speculators. Our monetary transactions are more and more virtual, without a real flow of money. That is one problem that not only the financial markets but also different governments must confront.

The other problem is our attitude to money. We need it in order to live, but we are not living just to earn as much money as possible. Money always serves human beings, and it ought to serve nature and its perpetuation. When we earn money by exploiting Creation, that is bad money that is anti-nature. We must put money at the service of nature, and not plunder nature in this way.

The thought of money triggers something different in each individual. For one person it brings memories of how she never got her fair share as a child. Another will feel greed; he can never get enough because he must fill his inner emptiness with money. For this reason, human and spiritual maturity are needed to be able to deal appropriately with money. Money serves the lives of human beings, so it should never become a subject in its own right, but always be placed at humanity's service. Only then can it be a blessing rather than a curse. Money should never become the highest value, whether for an individual, a society, or a company. When we talk about the value of money, this means something different from the values of Greek philosophy or Christian tradition. Values uphold human dignity, and the individual embodies values—you could say that a person who lives according to a particular value *is* that value. The value of money, on the other hand, is measurable. Money *has* value but it isn't itself a value.

CHAPTER 5

ACTING ETHICALLY

With an Introduction by
Jochen Zeitz

Toward the mid-1990s, as I was concentrating on the financial recovery of our company, my vice president and deputy Martin Gänsler was already urging me to rearrange production and designate someone to be responsible for the environment and social aspects. He suggested adjusting our methods and work systems as we went along, to better take into account environment-related and social factors. PUMA became a pioneer in this area; we called our internal guiding standards "PUMA.Safe." "Safe" was an abbreviation for "Social Accountability and Fundamental Environmental Standards."

Early on, we addressed accusations raised against us by non-governmental organizations. Since 1999, we have ensured that we only manufacture in factories that guarantee health, security, and wages for employees in line with our "Safe" standards. Our ultimate goal is to raise wages in our factories worldwide for unskilled workers to a level that will provide a livelihood for them, education for their children, and the opportunity to build up savings in their country, thus ensuring a certain living standard for the whole family. Our "Safe" standards closely follow the

Universal Declaration of Human Rights of the United Nations, among other sources. The question remains: from an ethical point of view, is that enough for a financially strong company like ours to do?

I know that no single person, company, or government can be the perfect fit for society or restore the balance of the world. But those among us who want to change things can work on the most important problems piece by piece. Just as Nobel Laureate Desmond Tutu said when he urged people not to be discouraged by being a small part of a large dispute, "Remember that there is only one way to eat an elephant: one piece at a time."[1] Everyone ought to use his professional responsibility to do this, beginning by defining ethics within his personal surroundings.

ETHICAL GUIDELINES

Official ethical guidelines have been in place and implemented at PUMA, as in many other companies, for some time already. Often, codes of ethics and similar documents are read only once by the employees and then put away in a drawer. Even scandal-wracked Enron had a code of ethics. The problem in that case was simply that the executive personnel and the employees quite explicitly did not implement the code. I wanted to make PUMA into a kind of anti-Enron—a firm that tries to live its ethics every day and in every way.

It seemed important to me to set simple, understandable, high-priority ethical guidelines and principles for our company: fair, honest, positive, and creative. These four key words, which we call the "Four Keys" (or 4Keys), serve as our foundation. Put into practice simultaneously, they lead all our decisions, transactions, procedures, and business practices. We have defined them as follows:

- FAIR

    At PUMA, fair means balanced. It means we see both sides, and resist the pressures that can push us into extreme ways of thinking, working, or living. It also means we are open to all, and refuse to discriminate against people or make judgments based on gender, race, religion, political persuasion, sexual preference, or way of life. And being fair means listening as much as we talk, and giving back as much as we take.

- HONEST

    Honest means sincere. It means not faking it—and walking the walk as much as we talk the talk. It means putting our money, our time, and our energy where our mouth is. And being honest means admitting our mistakes, and owning up to our responsibilities—something that applies to companies as much as it does to individuals.

- POSITIVE

    Positive means constructive. It means building up things—and people—not breaking them down. It means suggesting rather than criticizing, and working for solutions rather than just complaining. It means supporting others when they try, encouraging them when they fail, and celebrating with them when they succeed. It means "we can" more often than "we can't."

- CREATIVE

    Creative means imaginative. It means thinking outside the box, or thinking outside the shoebox, as the case may be. Being creative means finding a way around a problem, rather than stopping when the walls are too high. It means looking at new ways, listening to new ideas, and trying new strategies. It means striving for the most innovative solution because just being good enough is never good enough. Being creative means having dreams, and then making those dreams real things, in our individual worlds, in the PUMA world, in the real world.

The 4Keys apply as much to the decisions and actions of the CEO as they do to our retail team members who interact with our customers. In fact, it applies to everyone in our company. Eventually, PUMAVision and its guiding compass of the 4Keys will become an instinctive way of thinking for PUMA as we work toward making our contribution toward a better world.

In fact, these four key words are also decisive for my personal actions. They help me to scrutinize my thinking on an ongoing basis and to adapt. They will no doubt lead me in the future as well. I have the impression that something similar is true for many people in the company with whom I work closely. In fact, PUMA's majority shareholder, PPR, which owns some of the most recognized brand names in the luxury and sport and lifestyle industries, has now also adopted the 4Keys for the entire group.

Of course, I don't want to appear naive. Friedrich Nietzsche once stressed that ethics and morality can be completely subjective. Actually, every culture harbors values and ethical practices which are not compatible or even contradict each other. Nietzsche coined the expression *perspectivism* for this and maintained that we all find opportunities for asserting or even imposing our own moral ways of seeing vis-à-vis others.[2] However, there is also proof that many people aspire to common objectives such as justice and world peace, despite their cultural and personal differences. At PUMA, we identified peace and security, including secure working conditions for all employees, as important objectives some time ago.

We are not living in an ideal world. Often, managers must cut a process short by making decisions in the abstract at the company level. It is difficult to foresee the impact of this kind of macro decision on the micro world of departments and individuals. Good intuition, feedback from the people affected, and their integration into the whole are necessary here.

The definitions of our four key words was the first step, but this is only a small piece. Our PUMAVision doesn't really change anything in the overall critical situation of the world, especially when recognizing that we are unable to achieve some of our environmental and social goals in the short term as we are still operating within a single-minded financial system and drive for ever-greater financial profits.

THERE IS STILL MUCH TO DO

We are intensifying our efforts to abide by our ethical code on many levels by translating them into tangible actions and strategies that allow us to ethically grow our business while reducing our overall negative impact on the environment and, in some cases, on society. In our effort to reduce our environmental impact and the maintenance of social standards in production and worldwide sales, the derivation of our raw materials plays an ever-larger role. In the future we want to ensure that these become more sustainable and are grown or produced in a socially fair manner.

As a further effort to match our actions to our ethical code, our majority shareholder, PPR, invested on behalf of all of its brands (including PUMA) and acquired a 5 percent stake in Wildlife Works Carbon, LLC, an offsetting project in Kenya. The organization is the world's first REDD (reduced emissions from deforestation and degradation) program to be validated and verified for compliance with the voluntary carbon standard (VCS). Wildlife Works' business model reflects our mission at PPR through a multipronged approach of directly reducing greenhouse gas emissions. The organization protects threatened forests that are essential in mitigating climate change, improves the quality of life for local communities, and conserves endangered wildlife. Aside from already having 500,000 hectares under protection, Wildlife Works Carbon has a prospective project pipeline of several million hectares of natural forests around the world that they are working to purchase. The investment fulfills one of PPR's primary goals, to invest in for-profit businesses that incorporate biodiversity conservation and social concerns into their business model, resulting in net-positive social and environmental impacts. PPR now plays an active role in supporting Wildlife Works' aims to secure 5 million hectares of native forest over the next three years and to protect them for a minimum of twenty years with an expected 25 million tonnes of CO_2 emissions mitigated annually, while supporting human well-being and improved livelihoods for local communities. This investment should make it possible to make a contribution to species diversity and significantly reduce our net CO_2 footprint, in addition to the carbon offsets that we are purchasing on an annual basis and our targeted reductions.

It was also important for me to get involved privately with my time and money, beyond my activities at PUMA. That's why I founded the Zeitz Foundation for intercultural ecosphere protection in 2009. It supports private initiatives worldwide, such as companies involved in tourism and agriculture that conduct their business in harmony with environmental protection and the local community and its culture. In this way, I want to make my personal contribution toward preserving some spots on this planet for the future.

I assume in all this that even if we have no exaggerated illusions about our own significance, we can still combine our own light with other lights. Together, these lights ensure better visibility, more warmth, and more hope.

In the meantime, managers may realize that they have contributed significantly to major worldwide problems, and begin to give warning about these problems and help to tackle them effectively. We can and must take the lead by giving a good example of ethical trading—whether every man for himself, in groups, or with broader-based action. For me this action is an unconditional *must* today. Acting ethically is the key to a restful night and a good and fulfilling workday.

DIALOGUE: MANAGER AND MONK

ANSELM GRÜN: The fact that so many ethics commissions are springing up these days should give us something to think about, shouldn't it? These commissions are often concerned with medical or biotechnological questions, and they are concerned first of all with the question of what is allowed. It would surely do the economy good if business ethicists united and came up with ideas about the kind of ethics that should apply to all companies worldwide. However, the aim is not to have these ethics commissions control the behavior of the economy, but rather for them to raise awareness in companies about the standards they should follow in management, especially in handling nature.

By "ethics," philosophers mean methodical reflection about human actions, insofar as they are good or bad, required or forbidden. There are different approaches to ethics: one might examine the character of virtues, while another focuses on principles and standards. A third approach is related to ways of behaving in a very specific context. In this last sense, you can talk of professional ethics, business or economic ethics, and medical ethics. Each sphere of human action needs an ethical foundation. When a human being gifted with reason acts without reflection, his action will be beneath his dignity, for it is part of human dignity to consider our actions and examine and justify them with philosophical and theological arguments.

Philosophical ethics does not limit itself to the practices of the past. The ethicist asks in general terms whether a person's action lives up to the essence and nature of humankind. Without reflection, the individual would merely follow orders from others. Ethicists want to identify the Good and how we can acquire insight into it.

Consequently, the highest maxim of Greek philosophy (particularly of the Stoics) is "Act in accordance with nature." Because of this, ethicists are also interested in nature. We cannot know once and for all what it means to act in accordance with one's nature; it acquires new coloring according to the situation. When we speak of nature today, we don't mean the character of humans, but the nature that surrounds us, the creation of God. And we sense that ethics must always include environmental ethics as well. At the time when the Stoics constructed their system of theories, these issues were hardly in view, as humankind was still living in harmony with nature, for the most part. Environmental destruction was not yet a real concern.

JOCHEN ZEITZ: We need codes, principles, and guidelines for our ethical actions, but I must point out that law and rules are not the same thing as ethics. Laws alone cannot guarantee acting ethically, and they do not cover the entire spectrum of moral decisions which people have to make.

In most countries, the law leaves open many questions that are left to the personal decision of the individual. In addition, people deliberately break the law in many places on earth. Let me give a practical example illustrating this, one which many of us have seen or experienced ourselves: surveys show that citizens of many countries deliberately drive at speeds in excess of the legally prescribed speed limit. But those same citizens usually brake when they see people injured in a traffic accident and call to ask for help; or they stop to help the injured parties when help has not yet arrived. In some countries there is a legal duty to stop or make a request for help, and yet most people living there give such help because this is a humane and morally good action. But when they consider a law unjustified, as in the case of speed limits, then they simply ignore it, even when this is illegal.

Let's take another example, this time from the corporate world. Recycling is not legally required in many countries, but many of us involved in businesses consider it unethical to simply dispose of tons of reusable industrial waste as garbage. The laws may permit simple and easy methods of garbage disposal, but we cannot do this with a clear conscience and must see to it that we cause the least possible damage to nature.

ANSELM GRÜN: It may be that companies will need to set up their own guidelines for such situations. Yet these don't replace the duty of responsible individuals and employees to constantly examine themselves and question their own actions. We monks are intrinsically no better than the employees of a firm. There are employees of ours who work more rigorously and selflessly than many of my fellow Brothers. Even as a monk, one can get set in one's ways. But in essence a monk is someone who seeks God for the whole of his life, as Benedict describes this. At the human level that means that he doesn't stand still but is always seeking to be more authentic, to be more permeable to the spirit of God. He does not always succeed, for even a monk brings his life story along with him into the monastery and, all too often, that story includes wounds and scars.

Ethically speaking, I do not always succeed, although many people regard me as a moral authority. I don't see myself as a model, and I have never copied models. Nevertheless, there are people who have made an impression on me and aroused something in me which I wanted to develop for myself. One such person is

73

Henry J. M. Nouwen, the Dutch theologian and psychologist, who has fascinated me with his honest searching and sensitivity. There is the German theologian Karl Rahner, subject of my doctoral studies, who always put his personality on the back burner in favor of his work. And there are Brothers like my Master of Novices Father Augustine Hahner, who radiates great goodness. These people have sparked something in me, but they were also not perfect. They had their limits and weaknesses, and that makes them likable.

I sense in myself the danger that many people will project too much onto me. When they read my books, they think that I can solve all problems, that I have always been kindhearted and understanding in dealing with others, and that I am always in harmony with myself. I realize that I must protect myself against such projections, for they are not good for me. They idealize me. If I were to identify myself with these projections, I would become blind to my weaknesses and would come to a standstill. For me, it is important to be authentic. Authenticity means being entirely myself, searching to be more in touch with my true self and to live this outwardly, without letting myself be influenced by the expectations of others.

It is always dangerous when we hold ourselves up as an example, saying implicitly: "See here: you must also live like me." We can only strive to be honest and real, and keep working on ourselves so that the values for which we stand will light up in us. But at the same time, an attitude of modesty (which Benedict repeatedly calls for) is needed in order to stay grounded and avoid "taking off." We can only encounter people here on the ground. If we "take off," we are hovering above them. Then there is no contact—just a projection that really doesn't help. In encounters with others, we are being asked to consistently do justice to this particular person and also to the values we represent.

JOCHEN ZEITZ: Drawing on my own experience, I feel that a manager needs his own inner ethical drive and must allow it to lead him. He should also recognize that many people like to see executive personalities as models for ethical behavior. But a manager must see to it that he isn't regarded as an idealized projection. He is really "primus inter pares": first among equals.

I personally have not had any particular role models, apart from John Wayne in my youth. I find that inspirations and ideas for new procedures come from totally different contexts and from varied, humane ways of thinking.

ANSELM GRÜN: Firms with self-respect have more than guidelines and rules. Many have established foundations in order to support social or ecological projects, or, like Bill Gates, who has specialized in using his money to fight malaria, they have involved themselves in specific areas.

In Germany, the church tax serves to maintain not only priests and pastors but also many social institutions such as kindergartens, homes for the handicapped, and counseling centers. In this way, an individual's tax makes a contribution to the social and religious welfare of the population. Many Germans donate large amounts annually for social, missionary, or ecological projects. They feel that they want to share their wealth with others. That is their contribution to the welfare of mankind. The fact that they can help others with their money does them good and puts their consciences at rest. They are not giving to satisfy ethical instructions, but because they have a feeling in themselves that they don't want to keep their material possessions for themselves alone and must take on some form of social responsibility. Things will go better for the person who addresses his sense of responsibility for others in this way.

We monks receive no share in the church tax, but must support ourselves financially. From the profits that we earn by doing business, we donate to other monasteries in poorer regions of the world, to help them with development. We also request donations for particular projects that we want to carry out—in Africa, above all. We are supposed to earn our own livelihood ourselves, but with projects that we initiate for others, such as our schools or the cost-free therapeutic riding program for handicapped children at our facility, we ask for donations because we could not finance these services ourselves.

Where donations are concerned, we are not acting to satisfy an ethical principle but are acting out of solidarity with others, because their need concerns us. We are reacting ethically to the needs of others, of our own accord. But ethics alone is not a sufficient motivation; it remains abstract or "in the head," you might say. One also needs an inner sense for what is good, appropriate, helpful, and life-affirming.

Experience demonstrates that when we generously support others, then money returns to us from elsewhere. The person who always snatches up everything for himself and clings to it often loses it all again. The person who gives also receives. In this respect, what Jesus says corresponds to our own experience: "Those who want to save their life will lose it, and those who want to lose their life for my sake, and for the sake of the gospel, will save it" (Mark 8:35). Or consider what Paul wrote to the wealthier Christians in Corinth in his collection for poor communities in Jerusalem: "The one who sows sparingly will also reap sparingly, and the one who sows bountifully will also reap bountifully" (2 Corinthians 9:6).

JOCHEN ZEITZ: In the Bible it also says that one should give one-tenth: "Bring the full tithe into my storehouse" (Malachi 3:10). In my view that means that when things are going well for us and we have achieved balance, happiness, and perhaps prosperity, then we ought to share this with others who aren't in such a good situation. But the decision to give to others ought to be left to the individual, the institution, or the company concerned.

In principle, acting ethically is not tied up with money and cannot be measured in cash value, just as you cannot buy a humane life approach in the same way you would buy a chocolate bar. We can all live according to ethical principles without cost.

CHAPTER 6

THE ENVIRONMENT

WITH AN INTRODUCTION BY
ANSELM GRÜN

From the first pages of the Bible, in what is called the Creation Story, it is clear that Man has been placed in a natural environment. An earlier passage in the Book of Genesis (Genesis 2:4–25) relates how God put Man in the Garden of Eden to cultivate, develop, and protect it. So Man, too, has responsibility for the Creation and for nature. He is supposed to handle nature carefully and shape his environment to display the beauty which the Creator bestowed on the Garden of Eden. Humans should hold a protective hand over their environment. They are responsible for seeing that nature flourishes all around him.

In a later Biblical text we find the quotation that is sometimes misunderstood in Christian tradition as indicating the supremacy of Man over nature: "God blessed them, and God said to them, 'Be fruitful and multiply, and fill the earth and subdue it; and have dominion over the fish of the sea and over the birds of the air and over every living thing that moves upon the earth'" (Genesis 1:28). Yet these words do not sanction the exploitation of nature. They are concerned instead with the fact that Man's work carries forward the power of God's blessing to the rest of His Creation.

In other words, Man should manage his environment so that it will become a blessing for him and for itself.

In the New Testament, Jesus invites his disciples to look carefully at their environment. He intends that what we observe in nature should be a metaphor for our own lives. (That is still true today.) He refers to the birds in the heavens and the lilies of the field (Matthew 6:26–33), which are images for God's caring for us. So we should not live fearfully in this world, but live with the confidence that God bestowed on us at the time of Creation. The Creation has sufficient nourishment and clothing ready for us if we treat it well; we must not exploit it out of fear that we will not receive our fair share. Rather, our task is to manage Creation responsibly and fairly, so Man should let God rule over it and not raise himself in status to the Lord of Creation. Instead, we human beings should be concerned first and foremost with God's kingdom and his justice (see Matthew 6:33).

THE BENEDICTINE WAY: DEEP ROOTS AND PARADISE GARDENS

The Benedictine tradition has taken this seriously. Because Benedictine monasteries remain (as far as possible) in the very same place from the time they are founded—Benedict speaks of "stabilitas" and permanence—the monks are very committed to shaping their environment so that it will survive and be useful for future generations. Today we might label that "regionalism." Even in a globalized world, it is important to emphasize the economies of individual regions. When you build on regional strengths, this spares the environment. You are using resources found where you are, without exploiting them.

Rooted in the region where they are located, Benedictine monasteries support numerous relationships to people in their vicinity and offer them employment. The Benedictines look to what is nearby and want what they see to be well arranged. Yet as they carefully cultivate and preserve their defined surroundings, they are making a contribution to a more humane environment with a higher quality of life.

The Benedictines have shaped their environment in a manner that expresses their spirit—a spirit of praise and the spirit of respect for the Creator and Creation. For Saint Benedict, it was important to praise God the Creator daily. Whoever does this sees Creation with new eyes. He sees God's spirit at work in his surroundings and arranges them to praise the Creator.

Because of this spirit, aesthetics are also important in a monastery. The Brothers express the beauty of Creation by establishing gardens, for example. Space is left for nature there, but the monks express the beauty of the Creator in their own creations, too—for example, in the way in which they build their monasteries and decorate their churches.

But the aesthetic dimension isn't the only important feature for Benedictines as they shape their environment: considerations of healing are also important. Creation is full of healing powers, and to illustrate this the monks have set up herb gardens of mainly medicinal herbs. They have researched the efficacy of these herbs and utilize them in monastery medications—intended not only for themselves but also for the people of their immediate area. The monks also demonstrate their close relationship to the environment by teaching others a way of living that is appropriate to them and their environment.

The monks named the gardens inside their cloisters "paradise gardens." According to the earlier story of the Creation in the Bible, God placed Man in Paradise, in a Garden of Eden. It was only because Man abandoned God's order that he was driven away from there, but since that time he has carried the longing for a lost paradise within him. The monks brought this longing to life by creating harmonious, well-arranged gardens where humans, plants, and animals could coexist in a spirit of peace. Even today, these gardens are still places filled with calm and rich in beneficial scents.

A fundamental element of the monks' gardening and farming culture was their belief that they shared a common destiny with their environment. They regarded it as a sin to damage the environment through their conduct or immoderate practices. Because the monks knew themselves to be at one with nature, they were successful managers for centuries.

This seemingly old-fashioned type of management has something to tell us today in the time of global climate change. We will only be successful over the long term if we take our environment seriously. That applies first to nature but just as much to our human environment.

The monks were influential in the society in which they lived. Monasteries were the major employers in the Middle Ages. They anticipated modern pensions and health insurance with their own versions of both: health insurance was guaranteed by the monastery's herb gardens and medications, which were made available to employees and to the monks themselves. And because employees remained in the service of the monastery until the end of their lives, they continued to receive everything necessary for life, solving the problem of retirement insurance. Wages for employees consisted of money and payments in kind. Wages were higher during one's active working life, and then payments in kind were increased in old age.

A glance into history shows that the monks always had a good relationship with their human environment—not only with the employees of the monastery but also with the inhabitants of the monastery villages or monastery cities. We cannot return to this form of society today, but despite globalization there is a very healthy movement at present to reconnect and reunite worldwide and regional economies.

Grocery products should be regionally sourced in order to avoid transportation expenses, and the most important work—the skilled trades, above all—should be carried out by people from the immediate area. Regionalization and globalization are not contradictory, but they do need to coexist properly.

As missionary Benedictines, we don't focus solely on our own circumscribed environment. We are active worldwide. Our missionaries built monasteries in distant countries in order to put down roots, but they are rooted in their homeland at the same time. They facilitate education in Europe for monks from other parts of the world. In Münsterschwarzach we are in contact with monasteries in Africa, America, and Asia. This is a lively exchange, and in this way our perspective is broadened to take in the entire world. We don't want to simply export our lives to distant countries; instead, we want to shape the environment wherever we ourselves settle. And at the same time we want to learn from the cultures in which we are taking root. The dialogue with foreign cultures enriches our life: we sense this more and more in our monasteries in Germany and in other countries.

DIALOGUE: MANAGER AND MONK

JOCHEN ZEITZ: When you look at the internal development of a company and its relationship with the environment, businesses have a huge disadvantage compared with monasteries. The first Christian monks and the hermits in the desert lived over fifteen hundred years ago. As monks and their successors, you and your Brothers, Father Anselm, have had considerable time to test and adapt your lifestyle, your spirituality, and your idea of God. The desert monks actually were among our first psychologists, and they had a deep understanding of life and death.

In our present-day context, of course, the spirit of a business is not so profound or spiritual, even if it is built up over a relatively long period of time. The day-to-day competition of trade and commerce scarcely leaves time or space for other life dimensions. But for a business to be successful beyond the short term, it has to have its own spirit: it must have conviction about its products and what it stands for; it must develop a culture; and it must exhibit and live its own shared values. Without a positive spirit, a company will not be successful decade after decade, and definitely not for an entire millennium.

ANSELM GRÜN: In spite of—or perhaps because of—our long tradition, we also have to prove ourselves anew every day. In fact, monks try to arrange their surroundings to express their own spirit. But even monks are not always marked by the spirit of respect and love, conscientiousness and care. They are not always filled with the spirit of Jesus. This is why their demons sometimes find expression in the monastery and in their surroundings: when monks neglect the monastery spaces, for instance, or when they abandon austere frugality and furnish their cells comfortably; or when they lose their feeling for the aesthetic of their structures and take their cue from fashions they encounter on the outside.

Consequently, there needs to be constant reflection even in a community of monks about the kind of spirit which governs us and reveals itself in our buildings and our gardens, in our workshops and salesrooms. Sometimes a visitor's gaze helps to make us aware of the kind of spirit reflected in this or that space or in this or that patch of garden around the monastery. We need feedback from the outside in order to reach out with renewed energy for the spirit in which we are living and which we want to express.

JOCHEN ZEITZ: All the same, you are much nearer to nature than we are. The corporate world can lead us away from nature and the true feeling of home. To counteract this, some companies have chosen to locate their head offices where their employees can take a walk in a natural setting, meditate beside a spring, or devote themselves to gardening. The monastery garden provides a very special "inner" climate. You could say that it renews the agreement with nature.

Employers and managers often discover that nature is the best remedy against a hectic pace and burnout. That is why most business retreats—periods of withdrawing from commercial life—focus on spiritual and natural living. The garden of a monastery is often a place for listening, just like national parks and wildlife reserves.

ANSELM GRÜN: Yes, that's why I am happy and thankful that our monastery is in the countryside, where I have abundant opportunities to experience nature. There is the quiet path through the monastery garden whenever I am meditating by myself. There are a scant ten minutes following vespers—the liturgy of the hours in the church— which are an invitation to walk through the garden. In the course of this, I not only enjoy nature but also imagine how the trees were planted by monks who lived in this monastery long before me.

In the summer months, I often move my meditation into the open air. In the morning at 5:45 after early choir I go through our "Brook Avenue," a wonderful path along a stream and under old trees that monks planted in 1935 when the church was being built. There I hear the twittering of birds, taste the fresh scent of morning, smell the flowers and trees, and let the wind blow around my face and hands. That refreshes me and gives me the feeling of participating in the unending vitality of nature, which for me originates with God. In this way nature leads me to the source, which is God.

Next to the wide monastery garden there is also the cloister garden within the monastery buildings. Cloister gardens have been laid out with great care from time immemorial, and are called Paradise Gardens. They usually include a well with trees and flowers planted nearby. This garden reminds the monks of the paradise which Adam and Eve cultivated and in which they lived in community with God. It is interesting to me that the earlier monks didn't call their churches "paradise," but instead gave this name to their gardens. There they found some of the peace and harmony with Creation and the Creator which Adam and Eve experienced. When I go to the cloister garden today, I sense some of the security which nature imparts to us.

JOCHEN ZEITZ: Awakening this closeness to nature and spirituality in younger people is one of the biggest tasks of our time. Spirituality is deeply anchored in the human soul, and religions are the interpretation of this spirituality. Today there are virtually countless opportunities to experience spirituality. More and more people are searching and defining their entire personal spirituality within these possibilities. That they are increasingly less likely to find answers in a religion may indicate that some traditional religions perhaps need a better translation—a more current form of their communication and language. Today it is sometimes difficult for us to have access to traditional religious messages and relate to them because we often fail to understand them. In many cases they no longer move our consciousness. There are fewer and fewer people who take time to read the Bible and understand it.

To get more young people to explore their spiritual side, religion must interpret the spiritual and mythological images of the past, in terms of the visual concepts of the modern age, and transpose them to make them understandable and relevant. Art has changed over the course of time, as have music, literature, and language. The connections between people have changed: between men and women, between races and cultures, and in some cases between social classes as well.

Religious leaders must be open to each other in the face of these issues. I think that the liberal views of the Benedictine monks are very helpful in this respect, but there is also a challenge to the guardians of religion from an increasing number of liberal and modern rebels. That is why Eastern religions are rapidly gaining significance in the West, and this has become a lasting trend. We humans need balance, inner freedom, and guidelines in our lives. Religion can help in this regard when people understand it. Just as environmental activists have often had difficulties putting their message of sustainability into words, religions confront similar challenges today in communicating their message in keeping with the times.

ANSELM GRÜN: That is exactly how I see my mission: to formulate the wisdom of Christian tradition in language people today will understand. Just as you have pointed out, I sense a great longing for a spirituality that will help men to live well in this globalized world. The paths to this inner source are traditional ones such as meditation and prayer, quiet, church services, and the many personal or ecclesiastical rituals. Another central feature of this wisdom is discovering nature as a religious place, as a space in which we discover the source of the holy love that is flowing within us. And nature doesn't judge us: in nature we feel ourselves accepted, safe, and secure, in a state of belonging. The early Church had some idea of the wisdom of nature when they discovered nature-based religions and promulgated them. Instead of extinguishing these religions, they took them up. They fixed the most important feast days of the church year to coincide with the old heathen holidays, which were always connected with an event in nature. In this way, they took up the longing that linked humankind with living and dying in nature, and fulfilled it in the context of Jesus's work. Unfortunately, Christianity has neglected the connection to nature in the last three hundred years because of the rise of rationalism, and this has alienated many people. As a result, dialogue with other religions is important for me to discover one-sided leanings in my own religion and balance them out. My dialogue with Buddhism enabled me to rediscover the mystic elements and the connection to nature in my Christian tradition.

The second aspect of religion for the individual today is the fact that it brings him out of himself. Religion shows that Man doesn't live for himself alone, but is created and thus has responsibility for Creation and for his brothers and sisters. We encounter these two responsibilities right from the first verses of the Bible: "The Lord God took the man and put him in the garden of Eden to till it and keep it" (Genesis 2:15). And then God put the question to Cain which applies to all of us: "Where is your brother Abel?" (Genesis 4:9). God didn't find Cain's excuse, "Am I my brother's keeper?" (Genesis 4:9), acceptable. Yes, we are keepers of our brothers and sisters. We cannot simply live for ourselves but are situated in a society which must operate responsibly toward all individuals and toward the entire Creation. The Ten Commandments (or rather, instructions) are an aid to living in this world in a way that furthers human coexistence. The German word *Gebot* ("commandment"), which is not well liked, is derived from the root "bheudh" which means something close to "awaken" or "become spiritually active." This is the same root which we see in the word *Buddha*: the Awakened One. The Commandments are intended to open our eyes so that we will go through the world awake, as awakened ones, and can become a blessing to the world.

When religion brings both these aspects to expression in language which touches the human heart, then it will never become outdated but will reveal its fundamental power again and again. But this requires effort on the part of those who seek to live religion themselves and preach it convincingly to others. I am quite hopeful that in the future, enough monks will live in monasteries to show the world an alternative lifestyle. This can be a constant and visible encouragement to question one's own way of living and improve it.

JOCHEN ZEITZ: As you have already written, the mission of your Order extends beyond its immediate milieu to the whole world. Let me point out a basic similarity between religion and business: a manager tries to find new customers and new markets so that his company can continually have stronger sales of its products and its brand. Often the goal is to have a global presence—in other words, to establish branch offices throughout the world. To do this, we must think globally and act locally. In Matthew 28:19, Jesus says to his Apostles: "Go therefore and make disciples of all nations. . . ." Isn't that a global mandate as well?

Forget the Christian message for a moment and regard the whole matter from a rather amusing perspective: when

I make people happy with tennis shoes, or when I make them happy by taking away their fears with the help of religion, isn't a similar principle at work? A product is being sold in both cases. Whether rightly or wrongly, they both have to do with making people feel good.

Of course this is taking place at very different levels; yet in America, hamburgers and priests are offered for sale on television in similar ways. Billy Graham and other television preachers have sold religion and God, and made millions in this way. I don't wish to insult anyone, but I think that at least some religious brands have already become big business.

Now we can talk about the differences . . . The Bible also says: "For what is a man profited if he shall gain the whole world, and lose his own soul?" It is clear then that a company can credit itself with a victory when it reaches the whole world with its products; however, religion cannot be satisfied only with that. Religion focuses on the soul and the question of what you can give to the world, rather than thinking about what you can take from it.

In the final analysis, religion means reconnecting with God—or the gods—and it has to do with constructing a lost connection, whereas the business world is always concerned with initiating new relationships. Marketing, as used in the commercial sector, assumes that there is a fundamental relation between external products or things and happiness. Most religions assert something different. They say that happiness does not consist in having more but rather in learning to accept what one has and to be thankful for it—not just with respect to material goods but also with respect to talents, health, and relationships.

So although there may be fundamental parallels between various types of businesses and religions, the two are complementary in the end. When there is a question in the business sector of getting ahead at any price, then religion is definitely opposed. But business and religion can complement each other in a best-case scenario, and it is incredible when an opportunity arises to learn from each other.

I am glad that I can learn from you.

ANSELM GRÜN: It is very true that for both business and religion, global thinking means being present in all parts of the world, going out into the entire world and selling one's products or message. That is a similarity. The difference for me consists, however, in the fact that religion is not compelled to woo away the "customers" from the "competition" (other religions); instead it is obliged to preach the message of Jesus in such a way that everyone who is prepared to hear it can understand and accept it. We follow Jesus's call to a global mission because we are convinced that his message is a healing one for all people: that it comes to grips with their deepest longings and may liberate them from fears and excessive expectations. But we recognize that other religions also offer healing stability and good directions about leading a successful life. We don't regard it as our goal that all people should become Christians, but rather that Christian communities should live in all regions of the earth and become the "leaven" of this world. The job of Christian communities is to live in the spirit of Jesus so as to transform the world and fill it with greater hope.

In the nineteenth century, the mind-set of those directing the churches was similar to that of globally operating companies. They believed that they could only be successful if they converted as many individuals as possible to Christianity and accepted them into the church. They believed that adherents of other religions were lost for eternity. This gave the missionaries tremendous

91

energy. But we cannot think this way any longer today. It is not a matter of capturing each other's "customers," but a question of being a living example of the Christian message so that everyone, including the adherents of other faiths, will be touched by this and reflect on their own religions.

I have been in Korea and Taiwan, where Buddhists are considered the spiritual individuals and Christians distinguish themselves primarily through their social and sociopolitical engagement. In the dialogue between Christians and Buddhists, the Christians have rediscovered their spiritual roots and endeavored to live them. The Buddhists, on the other hand, have realized that it is not enough just to meditate for yourself; you must also be active in society and politics. This mutual enhancement is ongoing today.

JOCHEN ZEITZ: It is always salutary to examine the system in which I operate, and put things into perspective. Seen from an overall point of view, the global financial crisis and the climate and other environmental crises have clearly and undeniably illuminated the weaknesses and mistakes of our free market system—not to mention the weaknesses of those who misuse this system exclusively for their personal advantage.

The global child abuse scandal in the Catholic Church has laid bare some of the hidden weaknesses of the religious system. Even though it is always wrong and unjust to generalize and "throw the first stone," we must make an effort to look closely at the mistakes we make, learn a lesson from them, and then undertake the necessary changes.

We can also conduct our own "personal disarmament" at the individual level, similar to a dialogue between religions; fair, honest, positive, and creative conduct ensures that we don't appear threatening to other people. Sincerity is not only the best tactic but is also incredibly disarming with respect to one's own weaknesses. The missionary work throughout the world in earlier centuries had its dark side, as does the globalization of markets today. People have done much harm in both names. Globalization really has many fundamentally positive effects: it is gradually dissolving political and spiritual boundaries and bringing people everywhere in the world in closer contact with each other. In the professional world, too, new possibilities are emerging in education and the creation of revenue. But every benefit also has a dark side.

I think that we should come together as globalized people to work for a better world, not forgetting in the process our roots and backgrounds (biological as well as cultural and social), but protecting them. Local and regional customs and art bring an infusion of color and talent to the global painting, so they definitely must be kept.

For this reason, one of PUMA's programs includes support for artists and art exhibitions in establishing connections—at a regional level in Africa through the Creative African Network, for example, and outside of Africa through the Creative South American and Caribbean Network, with other regions to follow suit. It is a major concern of ours to acknowledge, appreciate, and support national cultural traditions everywhere our company operates, often to our own advantage as well.

One of the problems of globalization is that it is predominantly driven by the Western industrial nations, often at the expense of developing countries. Therefore globalization can also lead to the faster obliteration of species and the destruction of cultures and communities. Since the beginning of the global "conquest," the number of languages spoken in the world has declined by half. Of around six thousand common living languages, almost three thousand are in the process of dying out. If things continue at this pace, half of our living cultural inheritance will disappear in the course of one further generation.

Wade Davis, a Canadian anthropologist, regards languages in the same way that a biologist sees the variety of species. He says, "Different cultures portray different perspectives on life itself, inspired by morality and naturally correct. And these different voices become part of the higher repertoire which humanity has at its disposal to be able to overcome future challenges."[1] Variety, whether of species or cultural differentiation, balances and stabilizes systems. While recognizing the positive aspects of globalization, we must not continue to develop into a completely formless, generic world in which cultures disappear and life becomes increasingly monotonous and standardized. It is true that the extinction of species and cultures has always been part of the development of our planet, but the speed with which this process is taking place today is clearly not a healthy development. Thus, globalization means both winning and losing.

CHAPTER 7

COMMERCE

WITH AN INTRODUCTION BY
JOCHEN ZEITZ

According to oral tradition, when the Lakota tribe, a branch of the Sioux nation of the North American plains, encountered herds of slaughtered buffalo shot by European settlers, their elders wept. It wasn't just the lack of respect for life and the Great Spirit that evoked this grief, but also the unbelievable waste. Lakota chief Luther Standing Bear emphasized that his tribe, just like many others, would never have killed without having a use for the whole buffalo—from the horns to the skin and meat. They never harmed two buffalo when one would be sufficient.

This behavior embodies *management* in the best sense of the word: aiming for a specific achievement with a minimum use of resources and minimal waste production. It is ironic that business these days is so closely associated with images of excessive expenditure and indebtedness, environmental pollution, and exhausting of natural resources, when management really should contribute to minimizing all of these, if not preventing them outright.

In fact, business confirms the importance of the statement that "less is more." In an ideal case, business implies the most for the least, without outstanding debts. Since it first originated, management has also been closely related to the famous saying of Henry David Thoreau: "Simplify. Simplify. Simplify."

It has been increasingly forgotten in recent times that business can be the silver lining in the cloud rather than the dark cloud over society. Originally, the advantages of economic activity were quickly recognized. When someone first went through the neighborhood wearing a sandwich board that said "Potatoes at Max's farm: two cents per box," and a second individual carried a sign reading "Potatoes at Gretchen's store: one penny per box," they were both providing a helpful service to society. Those who could read knew where they could get potatoes, and they also knew that one supplier was offering a more favorable price, though not necessarily better quality. So advertising was originally useful, despite today's debate about deceptive marketing and oversaturation.

Commercial enterprises offered similar simple advantages in the beginning. Establishing a company, restaurant, hotel, mill, or factory meant freedom and the possibility to express oneself, while creating jobs and useful products for others such as clothing, food, and tools. In fact, the word *commerce* was originally connected not with the notion of institutional investors and the market, but with the way in which goods and income were exchanged and administered in households and monasteries. When the Sumerians and Babylonians developed what we regard today as major national economies, this resulted in a number of advantages for those who could select from a wider assortment of supplies and basic consumer goods. Soon others profited from the price system, an index of relative value with which buyers and sellers could compare costs and rank products.

Centuries later, the first well-known economist, Adam Smith, saw the exchange of goods and currencies on a grand scale as part of the natural order. For Smith, the markets were guided by an "invisible hand" so that supply and demand were perfectly aligned with each other. In the view of David Hume, a friend of Smith and, like

96

him, one of the leading Scottish moral philosophers, there would be positive results when society and trade were determined by personal goals and self-interest. Commercial as well as social advantages could be produced by the intentions and affluence of individuals.

THE HUMAN ELEMENT

By the early eighteenth century, an industrial world had developed in which power plays, greed, and corruption propelled an urbane, aristocratic network. Later on, many economists—among them Adam Ferguson, Karl Marx, Thorstein Veblen, and John Kenneth Galbraith—pointed out the particular dangers of modern business. These dangers have only grown over time: cutthroat competition, profit maximizing, conspicuous consumption, ruthless corporate growth, proliferation of garbage, class struggles on account of the division of labor, and the overall irresponsibility of people and corporations. From Karl Marx's *Das Kapital* to Michael Moore's film *Capitalism: A Love Story*, critics of unrestrained capitalism have exposed the inhumane aspects of the investment economy, as embodied in corrupt executives and scandalous businesses such as Enron and financial swindlers like Bernie Madoff.

On the one hand, needs are filled by consumer goods and services, even if these have been more specialized in the last few decades and more closely tailored to individual purchasers and specific cultures. Still, the demand for products quickly morphs into habit or greed. As psychologists note, sheer materialism and excessive consumption may be external conditions, but they are frequently the expression of inner drives, needs, greed, fear, or emptiness. Many people feel an urgent need to fill this nothingness through the act of shopping, and many consumers, far from waking up from this accumulation fever, appear to develop a kind of amnesia. They forget who they are, while the craving to keep piling things up grows stronger, and they identify themselves increasingly with the portion of reality that can be purchased.

This is why, in the twenty-first century, we are not only concerned with greedy manipulators who abuse commerce for their own dark purposes. Much more problematic are the treadmills on which we are running, sometimes blindly, as if we could find fulfillment through the products we are chasing after. But consumers will never be truly fulfilled, for they require constantly greater quantities of alcohol, caffeine, nicotine, sugar, and other substances to satisfy their cravings.

As if this weren't enough, psychologists have determined that advertising strengthens human dependency on products. The posters no longer say "Potatoes at Max's farm—two cents per box." Instead, they read: "Pringles: Once you pop, you can't stop." Buried in this slogan is the subliminal message that the advertisement no longer wants just to sell a product; it also wants to sell a craving. In the final analysis, a single potato chip yields hardly any profit. But when you can sell a brand or a dependency, this could lead to increasing profits over decades. A child who tries a cigarette once may smoke fifty to one hundred packs per year for the rest of his (shortened) life. Already by 1995, Michael Jacobson, founder and director of the Center for Science in the Public Interest, had written that the average American spends three years watching television advertising—and developing such cravings—in a lifetime.[1]

Managers should bear this in mind—and so should I. In spite of this, however, and setting aside for the moment our management's implications for the environment, I am convinced that where PUMA is concerned it is not harmful to market textiles or shoes if this contributes to people's fitness and lets them feel strengthened in their individuality. In this regard textiles and shoes are of course something different from tobacco and alcohol. All of us—managers, marketers, and consumers—are called upon collectively to deal more responsibly with the subject of consumer addiction.

A MODEL FIRM

Commercial activity has changed, and so has its constantly growing appendage called marketing. In the 1970s, the economist John Kenneth Galbraith maintained in his book *The New Industrial State* that the primary goal of multinational concerns is no longer profit but growth for its own sake. Growth means corporate power, an advantage of size, cheaper employees, and access to the resources of many countries. Furthermore, if growth is managed rationally, then stronger expansion and profits will mirror each other.

Today, companies have grown so exponentially that many people assume that corporations are more influential than governments. With this increase in influence, the commercial world has the potential to be a healthy or harmful catalyst. Companies can reproduce and enhance the worst or the best in a society. A firm can be a model for others—or it can be the rotten apple that transmits decay to others.

Today I see at least three important social fields in which companies should be active as models: ethics, awareness of responsibility, and sustainability. Through these areas they can make a better contribution to the world as a whole. These topics are so important that we have dedicated a chapter to each of them in this book. But it should also be noted that none of these three spheres nor the economy itself can be discussed in isolation from the others. You can manage with regard for greater sustainability, just as you can also be ethically correct and then assume greater responsibility.

What would happen if those involved in business activity adopted a stronger and more consistent approach with regard to ethics, responsibility, and sustainability? Business already contributes many good things to society: jobs, products, and services. How would it be if leading industrialists also cooperated now and then, considering their duties toward the environment and humanity instead of always just competing to maximize their profits?

Here is an example: in September 2009 PUMA and Adidas, as sporting goods producers and competitors, took a step toward each other. With a very reserved relationship and scarcely any contact between our companies in the past, Herbert Hainer, my then counterpart at Adidas, and I reached out to each other. On the United Nations International Day of Peace, which is observed annually on September 21 in more than 190 countries, our employees participated in a mixed soccer team in a friendly contest while some of the premier league football teams that we sponsor played each other as well. The Day of Peace is intended to promote nonviolent, harmonious coexistence—not only between nations but also in families and among neighbors, acquaintances, and colleagues.

In view of the earlier history of our companies, it seemed to be a good idea to observe this day together. A bitter, interfamilial conflict led to the division of the family business in 1946, followed by a split some years later into two competing sporting goods firms. This likewise split the inhabitants of the small town of Herzogenaurach into two camps, and the effects of this break were felt for decades. When I began to work for PUMA, there were butcher shops where only our employees shopped, and restaurants which only Adidas employees frequented. Although the embattled founding families had ceased to be at the helm some time before, there was still hardly any contact between the two companies, despite their physical proximity. I myself had seen my counterpart at Adidas just twice in seventeen years. He had indicated earlier that he was also interested in meeting, so he agreed promptly when I called him to suggest the peace initiative. It was a complete success for all participants. Since that day our relations have been palpably more relaxed and we have become quite friendly with each other.

Of course, for PUMA and above all for me as chairman of the board, it was always important to satisfy our shareholders. At the same time, I wanted to create a clearly defined PUMA-Vision. It was meant to serve as an all-inclusive business, social, and environmental model, which is why many people would be involved in the creation of this vision of our company. When administrators and employees feel competent and jointly responsible, then they are living their collective values.

In fact, one of the most important aspects of a company is the atmosphere in which one works. By its very nature, a climate of trust, creativity, security, frankness, caring, peace, and similar principles guarantees better business management. Of course you can easily be distracted from these things by management crises and the course of business events, but those qualities should form the company's overall essence, which always comes first. When the firm's atmosphere or climate ensures cohesion of the team, then you can see problems from a proper perspective and in time overcome them.

In the corporate world such notions of a social climate are often described with the phrase "Doing well by doing good." When companies commit to giving something back through philanthropy, making contact with the community, evolving their business practices and social and environmental framework, and caring for employees, they strengthen their network and thus create better relationships with the public and a stronger bond with their customers.

YOU REAP WHAT YOU SOW

"You reap what you sow" is a widely known article of faith. The metaphor of sowing and reaping stems from the Judeo-Christian cultural sphere, but there is a version of this same theme in almost every culture and religion. In the Eastern world the so-called law of Karma maintains that everything that one does or refrains from in this life will have a corresponding result in the next life. This is also expressed as "what goes around, comes around."

Whether you prefer Isaac Newton's scientific formulation of the law—that to every action there is always an opposite reaction equal in magnitude—or the religious versions of this iconic human experience, it is also the central point of an economic equation. In Ralph Waldo Emerson's variation, the law could be formulated thus: "You get the customer's answer (reaction) and success in proportion to the quality of the product or the service which you are offering (the action)."

This rule can be extended much further still: a country, a company, or a society will bring about the happiness and fulfillment of customers or citizens in proportion to the quality of the trade— or arts, or education, or other things—that it offers. Certainly a company can resist this law for a short time, but if it is corrupt, it will collapse sooner or later. This happened to the bankrupt firm Enron, whose leadership team systematically planned the highly creative falsification of its books for years, thus unleashing one of the biggest corporate scandals ever in the United States— until the bankruptcy of Lehman Brothers in 2007 exposed the systemic flaws of our entire financial market system by leading us into the biggest financial crisis the modern world had ever seen. Eventually, every action brings about an opposite reaction. But we have forgotten this law. Business after business and company after company have taken more from the Earth than they have given back. People expect the economy and companies to deliver more growth, quarter after quarter and year after year; but our planet is not growing, and our resources are dwindling.

The current harvest in the form of bailouts—emergency rescues—of collapsing banks, companies, and bankrupt national economies was just as tragic as it was foreseeable. Banks and the investment community have taken more than they have given. Junk bonds, financial derivatives, securities no longer supported by gold, and unimaginably high government debts, sometimes calculated with financial tricks—all these point to the fact that many sectors and governments (and not just the resource industries) have taken too much.

Unfortunately and irrationally, still more consumption is often suggested as the answer to this, to keep the economy growing continuously. I find it alarming when I hear from an internationally influential banker that in his view, the financial system will soon be just as driven by opportunism as it was before the recession. That's why the key for understanding the economy is the knowledge that it cannot exist alone as "the economy." Nothing can exist in a vacuum; we forget that all too often. One cannot examine an organ outside of the human body without causing it to die. Likewise there is no commerce and economy as an isolated world; it only exists within the day-to-day realities of human life.

You can never fully and completely understand the economy and its underlying commercial activities in an isolated context, however brilliant a model you may use. Whatever a national economy, a company, a chairman of the board, or a citizen *gives* to humanity and the Earth triggers a positive reaction in the urban or global context. Whatever a national economy, a company, a chairman of the board, or a citizen *takes* will produce a negative reaction. Nothing and no one has been able to resist this law so far.

But it is not too late. There are cycles in the economy just as there are cycles in nature. We at PUMA will make an even greater effort, and we will have to completely change part of our thinking in order to learn how to manage better within the cycles and laws of nature. If our formulation of Isaac Newton's Law holds true, then all that we give—better products, better protection of the environment, better social commitments, better customer service—will automatically bring a positive cycle after it. To keep ourselves aware of this, it is time to measure profits and losses by a standard different from our existing financial standards. We must comprehensively raise the status of those profits and losses of Earth and the community which actually arise from our actions, our businesses, and the economy.

The American scientists Boyd Cohen and Monika Winn[2] point to different kinds of market failures as a possible explanation of why we are not currently quantifying environmental impact the way we quantify financial results. They say that although the proceeds of natural or social capital utilization are privatized, the actual costs are frequently not borne by the responsible individuals or companies, but rather by society as a whole. Moreover, natural capital is often undervalued by society, so that its members are not fully aware of the true costs of the exploitation of our Earth's capital. The connection between cause and effect is often obscured, too, which is why it is difficult for trading parties to reach well-informed decisions. These scientists close with the finding that—contrary to economic theory—many firms do not make optimum use of resources because they are caught in a "we've always done it this way" mind-set.

One way to create such a new approach, among other things, is to start incorporating the costs that result when we utilize and affect the natural capital of this Earth—that is, the natural resources that Earth puts at our disposal. For this we must learn how to measure, value, and balance the gains which we derive for our businesses and the growing consumer market from eco-services (that is, the services which nature and her natural systems offer us free of cost), and the damage that we cause. The calculation must include the real and complete expense to the planet and society, including the garbage that results because we only partially use natural products.

THE LIMITS OF THE MARKET ECONOMY

The free market economy has brought us many good things. It helps us to adjust supply and demand, and by supporting creative competition, it helps to improve products and services and maintain reasonable prices for the customer. People can feel free to be productively

active. The free market opens many opportunities to us as businesspeople and employees to develop our independent creativity
responsibly. We have the freedom to develop products and services,
shape lifestyles, build up a customer base, and make income.

But the free market economy also needs rules to effectively
implement certain findings. For all its power and vitality, the free
market economy is only a tool and servant. It is a bad master and
certainly no religion. For example, what is there, apart from rules
and laws, to make tobacco companies tell consumers the truth
about their tobacco consumption? And who, if not the regulators,
will tell the oil companies that they must become sustainable,
when they will not come to this conclusion themselves?

Though it may be tempting in theory, a free market without
rules is no more practical than a society without laws. If you consider the serious negative effects on many market sectors caused
by too much regulatory freedom, you have to ask why no systematic measures were taken to moderate this impact.

Traditional capitalism is reaching a burnout situation because
it operates by taking for granted constant growth, ever-available
resources, and a limitless supply of cheap labor and new markets.
This old capitalist paradigm was limited by what Donella Meadows, of MIT, and her colleagues call the "limits to growth"[3]: there
are limits to the debts that one can incur and the resources which
one can use, before the breath literally goes out of the system.

On the other hand, authors Paul Hawken and Amory and
Hunter Lovins of the Rocky Mountain Institute have postulated
a new industrial system with what they call "natural capitalism,"
based on totally different thought structures and values.[4] The
fundamental assumptions of this new eco-capitalism include
important findings: first, that the environment is not some small
conference venue for manufacturing products, but the shell in
which everything—products, personnel, resources, and economic systems—is contained. Second, economic development

is dependent on real, sustainable, natural capital—resources, in other words, which remain integrated in the continuous cycles and processes of Earth. Third, there is a problem with the economy if mistakes and human problems like avaricious management and abuse of the environment need to be corrected and eliminated in order to enable economic growth to become eco-friendly. Finally, the number of human inhabitants of this Earth is growing dramatically, which means that an overabundant "human resource" is emerging while the remaining resources of the Earth are declining in inverse proportion.

Just as a fish takes for granted the water in which it swims, we human beings unconsciously accept our natural capital as a matter of course: the fresh air, water, earth, minerals, chemicals, and natural systems and cycles necessary for life and a healthy economy. Only when it is just as prized and valued as economic growth and surplus capital can nature become an integrated and balanced component of the whole system we call Earth.

If we return to the basic idea of management as I described it at the beginning of this chapter, we realize that economic growth and nature cannot and may no longer stand in conflict with each other. Business and the environment can and must exist in a symbiotic relationship in the form of the new eco-capitalism. With eco-capitalism, it will be possible to use resources economically and have maximum efficiency in resource use as well.

To achieve these goals, one must understand the duty of care and the function of the market (aside from the free market's motive of watching for new business opportunities), and when and where it doesn't work or is wrongly used. The right measures must be specifically chosen with our economic system evolving; and in a best-case scenario, global rules and laws must be passed in order to help and reward companies to act in a more sustainable and holistic fashion while maintaining their energy and vitality while disincentivizing those who don't want to evolve. Corrective measures carried out by governments and nongovernmental organizations are necessary for this.

But this shouldn't mean that our ultimate goal is to stigmatize companies in order to get them to change their approach. If multinational corporate groups directed their enormous power and energy to preserving instead of superseding nature, what opportunities would arise! If anything can make companies and the economy recover and strengthen, then it is the renewed appreciation and the restoration of balance.

DIALOGUE: MANAGER AND MONK

ANSELM GRÜN: I am in agreement with you that the kind of pure capitalism that is only out for maximum profits and observes no rules is destructive for the future of our world. The financial crises showed what happens when capitalism sets aside values and only follows greed and extravagant demands for more earnings. There are more than enough people in the world who are ignoring the values described by the Greek philosophers and world religions, in order to have a competitive advantage. One would think that society would reject such people and refuse them opportunities, but unfortunately that is not the case, because financial capitalism is becoming ever more anonymous. You can boycott a firm that manufactures its products under inhumane production conditions and sells them with an advertising campaign contradicting human dignity. That company has no chance of lasting in the long term. But in the financial marketplace, customers often don't know who they are dealing with. For this reason, clear regulation is needed, otherwise destructive and disintegrative powers will be active in the sphere of the anonymous.

The financial crisis showed that we cannot manage without values, so it is our ongoing task to examine all our businesses for the values that underlie our dealings. In addition we must promote these values so that people sense that they are more important than short-term financial advantages.

Business must itself live those values that religions preach. Certainly religions—along with monasteries—have the duty of looking after people who are professionally unsuccessful, whose dreams of a fulfilled life are broken. But it would be too easy if they were only there to stick a "pious band-aid" on the wounds the economy has inflicted on them. The concern for those who have come up short, who are treated unjustly, should always lead to social and political action. Religions and the monasteries have the responsibility, derived from their experience in caring for defeated human beings, of seeing that the relationships in firms become more humane and that social structures are fair to people. Jesus gave us a prophetic spirit. This spirit expresses itself in the Old Testament through the prophets' denunciations of antisocial conditions and their appeals to justice. Today as well, churches have the duty to denounce structures and tendencies in society that hinder life and damage human beings.

JOCHEN ZEITZ: Without question, companies have a duty, and not only with respect to their treatment of current and discharged employees. They must also take to heart fundamental values to contribute to solving problems of overriding importance. We cannot expect governments to get rid of poverty in nature and society when the responsible parties are the economy and government in the first place.

As Paul Hawken rightly remarked, there are some important factors that must be taken into account here. First of all, the various economic sectors in many countries have set up influential lobbying initiatives which they increasingly support with all the means at their disposal. President Obama has pointed this out repeatedly—for example, in the framework of his comprehensive efforts toward stronger regulation of the financial markets. Second, many governments are only chosen for terms of a few years in office, so their thinking is often preoccupied with the next election. This limits their ability to bring about real change. Third, we have made it customary to hand over regulatory policy functions to the state as a neutral mediator, but this no longer works well in the age of globalization. Finally, every nation has its own vested interest in not putting excessive strain on its own companies. Great Britain doesn't want strict regulation of the finance markets, for example, because too many jobs in London depend on them. The United States protects the interests of its oil and agricultural industries; Germany rejected stricter environmental standards on behalf of its automobile industry, particularly where luxury vehicles are concerned; and Japan wants to protect its catch quota for red tuna against the demands of the species protection organization. As a result, it is still barely possible today to implement anything more than minimal standards in an international context. Because of this, global markets need global supervision without regulatory loopholes. Yet I hope that these restrictions will not always prevail. I hope that new ways of thinking and awareness of what we are doing and how we ought not to do it will find their way into election debates, just as they ought to find their way into boardrooms around the world.

109

In our present-day world, however, the limits of political power were all too apparent at the Climate Conference in Copenhagen at the end of 2009 and the follow-up event in Bonn in the summer of 2010. The result of these conferences (really not a result at all) is the triumph of self-interest over public interests. Nonetheless, a genuine global awareness was created for the first time in Copenhagen which (I believe) led to an irreversible trend that will develop further over time; this was also picked up by the Rio+20 conference in June of 2012. I believe that one day in the future, it ought to be the law for every company to carry out its business sustainably. Then when the company cannot manufacture a product with cleaner, greener, "cradle to cradle" sustainability—that is, in a circular economy without garbage and waste that cannot be reutilized by anyone including nature—it will receive no permission or at the least have to pay a fee or otherwise compensate for its negative effects to manufacture that product. I imagine a future society in which a company will not receive a license to be active at all if it cannot manufacture a product without exploiting people and resources. Everything we do, everything we manufacture and consume, and every way in which we generate and consume energy will be based on this new paradigm— green, clean, and sustainable. The collaboration of a responsible government with an ethical, sustainable business community is absolutely necessary for this. However, it must be based on a new way of doing business instead of regulations that just plug a few holes.

ANSELM GRÜN: The results of the Copenhagen Conference and Rio+20 were disappointing for me, but I still haven't lost hope that it was meaningful. The governments of different countries clearly recognized what happens when each of them only follows its own vested interests and lobbyists are merely out for their own advantage. They pointed out the limits of the global conversation. But I am confident that just this concession of defeat will open up a new power to face common problems together.

My view of religion plays an important role in this regard; it changes my positioning vis-à-vis the world and my own managing. We need a shift in thinking in this connection. Jesus called it a turning back. The Greek word for returning is *metanoeite*. It actually means "rethink, think differently, consider the other side of your actions, consider the results of your behavior." Sometimes it requires a breakdown to make us really turn back and rethink. When our discussions are always successful, we are in danger of settling into our own thoughts of success and overlooking much that must be considered. To get governments to talk differently with each other, much must change, particularly in the heads of voters. They can no longer think only about their own advantage, but must also have responsibility for the entire world in mind when they go to the polls in the future.

JOCHEN ZEITZ: Why should companies of the future not cooperate more strongly with each other in matters of the environment and social issues, pooling their strengths toward a common goal? At least once, one should grapple seriously with the question of whether there couldn't be a common movement of companies and their leaders: a "United Corporations or United Business Leaders for a Better World." I firmly believe that cooperation is possible. There have always been skeptics; one shouldn't allow oneself to be discouraged by them. I am certain

111

that people said the idea of the founding of the United Nations was naive. They cynically spread gossip that this organization would soon disband itself, like the League of Nations after World War One or the European Union in its crisis today. The Wright brothers had to listen to talk that their idea of "flying" with metal and canvas wings was absurd. Religious skeptics told them, "If God had wanted man to fly, he would have given him wings." Many ideas catch on in small ways before they become larger or "take off." A spark can kindle a gigantic bush fire. Sometimes it takes only a simple handshake to change direction in a long history. In any case, there is no doubt that cooperation and dialogue are necessary in today's world.

The same is true of optimism and persistence: you can start small, but not starting at all is no alternative. Many companies will refuse to deploy their energies creatively and will simply waste them in resisting change. Why not commit oneself to nature? I believe that there can be not just individual but also shared solutions, so long as they transcend borders and are inclusive and open, and not only supported by national interests. Take the Sustainable Apparel Coalition as it is called, for example. It is "an industry-wide group of over sixty leading apparel and footwear brands, retailers, suppliers, nonprofits, and nongovernmental organizations (NGOs) working to reduce the environmental and social impacts of apparel and footwear products around the world."[5] The coalition, which (in addition to PPR and PUMA and many of our large competitors) includes organizations such as Patagonia, Levis, H&M, and Inditex, cooperates and shares intellectual property that can lead to innovative, new business solutions.

PUMA also creates possibilities for collaboration with nongovernmental organizations, artists, and filmmakers in order to support projects such as social and environmental documentary films. So it is not naive to assume that companies can cooperate. It is far more naive to assume that the old isolationist company paradigm will help our planet.

One thing I have learned and respected in my life is this: if you don't try something, it simply won't happen (unless somebody else does it). Regardless of how large or small the idea, you must at least try out new things. Like life, every new idea is a trip, and you don't know where it will lead you. For me it is an adventure and a discovery every time.

ANSELM GRÜN: Unfortunately, it is customary at most firms to keep your strengths and company secrets to yourself and hope for a competitive advantage from this. Yet there have also been a number of positive exceptions in the past. In the nineteenth century, Friedrich Wilhelm Raiffeisen founded a cooperative association. He had realized that farmers have an advantage when their products are sold collectively and they can use the resources of the collective (both the credit of the cooperative bank and shared purchasing) for themselves.

We need new models for our time of how firms can cooperate. The shared search for sustainable methods of production is good for everyone. But companies can only cooperate when they are influenced by the same ideals and their businesses are not run at the expense of the other parties. That calls for the attitude which religions preach: not putting one's own ego first but rather the goal, for whose sake self-interest steps back into second place. When companies are dealing with a common goal of preserving Creation, then they will also be able to conduct themselves together in the face of those who (as always) manage without regard for sustainability. And they will bring about an atmosphere that permanently undermines the foundations of firms which act ruthlessly. They will shape the world together, and in the final analysis everyone will benefit from this.

JOCHEN ZEITZ: That may apply just as much to the interplay of business and religion. I absolutely believe that both worlds can benefit from each other, that belief and consumption do not unconditionally exclude each other. Up to now, however, they have frequently developed at each other's expense. Belief can certainly have a positive as well as a negative influence on the nature of our consumption. Without belief, consuming can become a religion in its own right, which is not helpful. Ideally, belief and consumption would complement and balance each other. Obviously certain consumer behavior can turn into an addiction and an uncontrolled breakdown of resources. That is why I would not defend excessive consumption, which also leads to illness and many other problems in society. On the contrary, I support a healthy balance between the material and spiritual spheres, for this leads in the end to greater health. After all, we don't want to hold back the gifts under the Christmas tree (or gifts of Hanukkah *gelt*, or similar traditions in other cultures) from our children. It's not a question of removing the material world, but of communicating a powerful feeling of magic and the memory of something larger with such gift giving. Aristotle spoke out in favor of the Golden Mean in life. By that he meant that we should choose the middle way between lack and excess in our lives. As an example, excessive reproduction leads to overpopulation, though no reproduction would mean that our species would totally disappear. In the same way, an excess of consumption leads to obesity, addiction, and further ills, yet a lack of consumption means anorexia, hunger, and ascetic misery.

Material commodities were given to us to enjoy, not for their misuse.

ANSELM GRÜN: At first glance, belief and consumption appear to be real opposites, for belief always includes asceticism. But asceticism doesn't mean that one denies life and enjoyment. Doing without, Sigmund Freud said, leads to the development of a strong ego. The person who must immediately fulfill every desire will become a slave of his own needs. Not much life will radiate from him, and he may eventually be unable to enjoy life or eating. You can only enjoy things in a lasting way when you can also do without them.

Joie de vivre and enjoyment absolutely belong to belief. This is shown in the Old Testament accounts where eternal life is described as a happy celebration with rich dishes and old wines. The conduct of Jesus, who was no typical ascetic, also demonstrates this. His opponents even called him a glutton and "wine guzzler" because he ate and drank with the publicans. Yet Hildegard of Bingen, the medieval mystic and nun skilled in the art of healing, says that discipline is the art of always being able to be pleased.

There are certainly movements within Christianity that emphasize poverty and focus on it so strongly that it becomes a denial of life. Saint Benedict talks about simplicity and economy rather than poverty. Fasting and abstaining belong to belief but so does celebrating—during the great festivals of the church year, for instance. The monastery culture itself generally stimulated production in the Middle Ages with building activity as well as its refinement of dining and the production of ingredients that went along with this. Monks grew grapes and brewed beer. Benedict always warned about excess, however. In his view, a monk can only enjoy himself in a lasting way if he is also prepared to observe periods of abstention such as the forty-day fast period.

Where growth is concerned, we should aim for moderate qualitative—not quantitative—growth. This is true also for products that we acquire. It is not very beneficial when we continually buy things in order to fill our homes with them. Only that which gives us joy or makes our life more worth living is really good for us in the long term.

CHAPTER 8

SUSTAINABILITY

WITH AN INTRODUCTION BY
JOCHEN ZEITZ

I wonder whether there will still be living species in 150 million years (the same length of time that separates us from the dinosaurs) and what they will say about us. Will they ask how many species that were still familiar in the twenty-first century have died out? Will we ourselves possibly be among those extinct breeds? Will the intelligent life forms of the future (highly developed, no doubt) be similar to us, if only genetically? Will they regard us as the problem species that caused the ship of life to sink? Or will they see us as the generation that finally came to its senses and reversed the ship's course?

We can assume that the dinosaurs couldn't foresee or prevent their own extinction. In contrast to this, future life forms will be obliged to establish that the human species recorded and published data like those set out below—and that in spite of this, they didn't do anything in time to prevent their own downfall. It is clear that our civilization is in danger. The population explosion, the Greenhouse Effect, ozone holes, the economic north-south divide, regional famines, wars, the plundering of mineral wealth, and severe damage to the ecosphere are all signs that humanity is taking a real beating.

Ironically, the human species, which so passionately collects data, knows about these dangers in precise detail. It would be a great mistake to wait and see just because scientists and lobbyist groups are arguing about forecasts, numbers, and their interpretation. The experts will never come to an agreement. Our environment is in danger and the time to act is now. As we go forward, there will always be new findings and we will need to adjust our actions accordingly. In management, you work according to the method of trial and error. We must also allow this principle to be applied responsibly in the case of environmental protection when something changes or improves. It is important to act and to make a start in areas where positive results have been achieved already.

Consider the following statistics, taken from *Home*, a documentary film by Yann Arthur Bertrand, who looked into the situation of Planet Earth and its inhabitants in 2009.[1]

- Twenty percent of the human population consumes 80 percent of the Earth's resources.
- The world spends twelve times as much for military objectives as it does on developmental assistance.
- Five thousand people die every day on account of polluted drinking water.
- One billion people have no access to clean drinking water.
- Almost one billion people suffer from hunger.
- Forty percent of the world's arable land has suffered lasting damage.
- Thirteen million hectares of forest disappear every year.
- Every fourth mammal, every eighth bird, and every third amphibian is threatened with extinction.
- The extinction of species today is happening one thousand times faster than it would through natural evolution alone.
- Three-quarters of fishing grounds are exhausted, either fished out or dramatically diminished.
- The polar ice caps are 40 percent thinner than they were forty years ago.

- The number of people forced to leave their place of habitation due to climate changes could climb to at least two hundred million by the year 2050.

What would happen if our governments and multinational corporations accepted a vision of mutual reliance and adopted it consistently? In many countries and companies we would have to develop further as we went along, so that we would strive not just to get into the black, but also to be green in the way we operate. After all, we didn't hesitate to invest hundreds of billions for the salvation of our global financial system and the stabilization of the European Union by financing Greece and now also other European countries. How much could we do if we were to spend the same amount for the salvation of our planet? Why is this approach not a feasible and realistic objective today, given the dramatic environmental problems that exist?

I believe that a comprehensive approach to sustainability is of decisive importance today. No group by itself, whether the financial elite, a political party, or a scientific think tank, has the answers to all questions. Those who remind us about the original solutions from history have come to this same conclusion: we all must bring about necessary, wide-reaching changes.

Aware of the importance of supporting recognition of global dependence, our PUMAVision reflects our relationships as people and as a company to our global family of living species. This entails first of all supporting a dialogue with others, and then letting others inspire us. As mentioned earlier, this corporate vision also includes our striving for a world that is at peace and in balance. The key values and practices of PUMA resulted from our wish to create higher standards for our products and our operations, not only in our own firm but also beyond its boundaries. So we find ourselves now in an ongoing process of trying to monitor and improve every aspect of our value chain, creating more transparency along the way. This extends from our sources for purchasing raw materials to the practices with which we protect our employees, to make sure that we are supporting and preserving life. But I know that this is only a beginning. We are inspired by the idea of a better world, which is still a long way from becoming reality.

DIALOGUE: MANAGER AND MONK

ANSELM GRÜN: It is time to act; you are right about that, Mr. Zeitz. That is going to require the energies of as many people as possible from both our worlds. Religion and business are truly the biggest formative forces in a society. With the culture which it creates in its companies, business influences the culture of society, too; and religion influences many people, not only as individuals but also in their lives with others. Today there is hardly a country left where a single religion sets the tone of the whole culture, even though in some regions, the year is still determined by the holidays of the church year. In most countries, for instance, Christmas contributes significantly to boosting the sales of retail chains and the larger economy.

Business and religion are essential for human beings: on the one hand, a person must earn a living, and this makes him essentially a commercial individual. On the other hand, people also feel a longing within for more, for a dimension that transcends this world. This is the longing for God and a longing for nature to be suffused with divine power and divine love—to be even more than just nature. The religious dimension confers dignity upon humans because they experience themselves as a son or daughter of God. And it bestows on us the feeling of security, of being subsumed in a larger context, in God's love.

In the final analysis, sustainability needs a religious dimension. Of course we can deal with nature in a sustainable fashion purely on rational grounds, because we would not survive otherwise. But pure reason is not a sufficient motive for managing sustainably; we have seen that in the last thirty years. The religious dimension is required to see nature as something holy, as something that is separate from our initiatives because it is created by God and imbued with God's presence.

It is the duty of all religions today to take up the cause of sustainable management. We are not talking about religions battling with each other, but about a common struggle to deal with each other and with Creation in the spirit of solidarity and love. If religion loses its power, then purely secular spheres of influence acquire a religious dimension, and that is not good for humanity. For example, when health is saddled (so to speak) with religious concepts—it seems to be the "highest good" today—then a religion of health evolves that is often very aggressive and demanding, and makes people fearful. Only when religion pervades all spheres of life such as health, business, the connection to nature, and human interrelationships, will people deal with these spheres in a fitting and healthy manner.

JOCHEN ZEITZ: Religion may be one means of bringing these questions together. But people must also understand independently from religion that the spheres of life that you mention—nature, business, society—are all linked with each other. Many of us do not yet understand this. I would like to give you an example. For the past seven years PUMA has organized a conference to which we invite different interest groups and stakeholders: colleagues, investors, environmental groups, NGOs, and business partners.

121

In the beginning, this conference was mainly a meeting at which the social issues of concern in our factories, such as wages and employee rights, were the main focus. To a lesser extent it was also concerned with the environment, but mainly with regard to employee health in our factories. Since 2009 we have included representatives for all three elements of our PUMAVision: peace, the environment and social security, and creativity. We no longer concentrate primarily on employer-employee relations or the protection of employees but instead look at our opportunities and take steps toward a better world in a broader, comprehensive context. One participant asked why we had to think about the environment, peace, or art, given that our concerns and problems are exclusively of a social nature. Certainly this man is right: we can still improve things in that area, and must; but we can no longer concentrate exclusively on one area and ignore another one in the process.

For companies, that means that we must expand on the original idea of Corporate Social Responsibility (CSR) by compellingly incorporating environmental protection (among other things) into our economic decisions.

Whether CSR is sufficient to solve the problems that the economy creates depends on how open, sincere, and far-reaching the CSR program itself is. Essentially, a good CSR program or project should help to prevent or head off those problems caused by commercial activity. This assumes that CSR is no longer just an initiative at the departmental level or a piece of window dressing, but an essential component of a company. When CSR is part of the company structure in this way, then the overall company strategy is based on a sustainable business model that can solve problems effectively and also identify new opportunities. So we need a comprehensive view of things, even if this often raises more questions than there are answers. Spirituality, religion, and metaphysics come into play here. Every part of the puzzle reflects the others and connects itself with them as in a hologram.

The business world has gone its own way for a long time in isolation from spirituality; often a kind of wall separated these two worlds. Why shouldn't we someday be able to remove the wall between natural science and religion, business and spirituality, monk and manager? I know that a manager can open his heart to the spiritual dimension just as I know that you, Father Anselm, can be a successful businessman and manager—in fact, you already are.

ANSELM GRÜN: I have been a manager for thirty-four years in my role as Cellarer of the Münsterschwarzach Abbey. The Cellarer is the financial administrator of the abbey: I have responsibility for just under three hundred employees and direct the roughly twenty trade businesses of the abbey; and I am the financial manager as well. That is a wholly worldly type of work in many respects, but for me it is simultaneously a spiritual duty, for I sense that my way of dealing with my colleagues and the way the abbey is managed shape the climate in which our employees work. It is a challenge for me to spread an atmosphere of peace and trust and hope. On the other hand, it is my job to awaken in the employees a feeling for coexistence and for new forms of managing—and for sustainable management as well. I know cellarers who hide themselves behind their money, and all too often they use this as a means of exercising power. That is a temptation that every boss is familiar with. It is all the more important to support colleagues instead of wielding power over them; to awaken life instead of proving oneself.

123

Those are all spiritual attitudes that even a cellarer doesn't acquire naturally but must practice constantly, in all humility.

Sustainability is very close to our hearts. We are certainly quite a long way from dealing in a completely sustainable fashion with our own energies and the resources of nature. Yet we have at least reached one of our objectives already, namely to obtain all our energy from renewable sources in the region by the year 2015. In the course of this, we produce more energy than we need: 14 percent more heating energy, all told, and a surplus of 40 percent of electrical power. Our next project is the conversion of our fleet of cars. Here again we want only cars that can operate on rechargeable energy. But none of the solutions offered today—hybrid cars, electric cars—have convinced us yet. So we try to achieve the best possible solutions with conventional automobiles. But we sense that we must be more creative in this area.

Our workshops are certified. We try to keep environmental aspects in mind—to treat the environment considerately, to produce as little environmentally damaging garbage and waste as possible. Certainly there is still more to do in this respect.

In our monthly building meetings, we discuss what sustainable management is. When we renovate or construct new buildings, when we produce furniture, when we renew electrical wiring and install lamps, it is important for us to consider sustainability in these ordinary tasks. Creating sustainable furniture often costs more, and building sustainably is often more expensive than conventional methods. But this pays off in the long term, for our buildings last significantly longer than comparable structures built by the province or communities. Our school building is already fifty years old. The ongoing renovations—improved windows, which waste less energy—result in only minimal costs compared with the high costs of a total renovation that public schools swallow up. Another area which we want to take on actively (though we have not achieved great progress here) is that of ecological cultivation in our fields and gardens, and the reorganization of our diet connected with this. We have the advantage of raising most of our foodstuffs ourselves. This does away with the whole question of packaging waste. But converting to whole foods and a significantly more vegetarian diet is a very sensitive subject which one cannot simply legislate from above. We are on the verge of awakening new awareness in our monastery, including among the employees in the kitchen, bakery, butcher facility, and farming and market gardens. We cannot rest complacently on what we have achieved so far, for new fields are always opening up in which we must rigorously follow through with sustainable management. The fact that we Benedictines always stay in the same place calls for sustainability. We want to shape our location in such a way that monks in later centuries will also feel at home here. So we plant a new tree for every one that is felled. The type of tree is determined in consultation with the beekeeper, to enable the bees to furnish good honey. We get our water from our own well, so we must handle fertilizers carefully in order to maintain the high quality of the well water.

JOCHEN ZEITZ: I have to say that I was surprised at how long your monastery has been cultivating a comprehensive, sustainable lifestyle. Father Anselm, you were good enough to take me in as a monk at Münsterschwarzach for a time in the summer of 2009. As you have already said, monks observe the principle of sustainability by growing their own foods as much as possible and concerning themselves with their environment. Monks cultivate and preserve their garden entirely in the sense of Biblical tradition. I recall what a strong contrast to my own lifestyle the life in your community presented at the beginning: getting up before five o'clock every day, praying five times per day, three communal meals taken in silence. In the first few days, before I adapted to the rhythm and found myself, it made me truly tired.

I was thankful for time in the monastery to reflect and to concern myself with the great existential questions that we often avoid in life—among others, the meaning of freedom, death, isolation, and the sense of life. And I also had some special questions that I wanted to ask you, Father Anselm, when I took this time out to reflect, such as: where do God and psychology come together?

One point easily forgotten in our hectic urban life is what I like to call the art of living. In a monastery one discovers again what it means to eat properly and register the taste of food with real intensity—partly on account of the rule of silence during meals. Beer was only allowed on Sundays, and it seemed to taste much better because we looked forward to it and then enjoyed it—and normally I don't like beer at all.

The art of living is difficult to experience in an era in which everybody talks about going faster, something I also experience daily. Among other things, the atmosphere of the cloister garden taught me that I must slow myself down sometimes in order to better sense the rhythm of my life. The blurring of life disappears when one can experience even small pleasures as such.

When I ran off to go jogging every second day, it was no longer all about identifying my speed and time and my pulse rate. Instead, I said to myself, "Hey, friend, go slowly and don't leave your soul behind!" I chose a different route every time in order to explore the beauty of nature around the monastery.

I experience something similar each time I look at the starry heaven at my farm in Kenya. Once I came back from a safari during which I had not been able to take a shower for a whole week. Suddenly I experienced a shower in a completely new way: as a precious, unique experience. So today I try to avoid taking for granted the transient pleasures of life.

I have the feeling that what you, Father Anselm, and your community can give to me and many others is of essential importance for our world. We cannot fix a broken world if we ourselves are broken. There can be no sustainable network without sustainable component parts. We are among the important components in a higher ecological system, and our own components—spirit, heart, and above all, soul—must be healthy so that our world can be healed in a sustainable way. For this reason I consider your work, Father Anselm, as not only complementary to mine but essential to it. Many thanks.

ANSELM GRÜN: Managers like you are not the only ones who can learn from us, and we also learn from companies. When I was at PUMA for an entire day and personally witnessed a worldwide teleconference about goals for the next year, I was very impressed at how clear and goal-oriented it was. Everything goes somewhat slower with us. That can have advantages, but sometimes we are ponderous as well. The main thing that became clear to me that day is that sustainability is not only an ideal that we honor in the monastery as at PUMA, but that sustainability is calculable, and it must always express itself in concrete objectives for areas such as packaging, transport, office work, and migrant labor. For everything that we do.

127

The management committee of PUMA named exact percentage figures and amounts in Euros which they wanted to save in energy and garbage. We have not thinned out our management divisions so precisely, so I drove home from PUMA stimulated to go through our different spheres little by little, in order to push for more sustainability and formulate clear goals.

JOCHEN ZEITZ: To begin with, we at PUMA formulated a clear and complementary mission in which sustainability has become a fixed component of our company guidelines: we want to become the most sought-after sustainable sport lifestyle company. Thus sustainability is anchored in the DNA of our brand and company. We defined a long-term action program on this basis with ambitious goals which we want to reach by 2015. I would like to set out just some of these goals in the environmental sphere:

Reduction of CO_2 emissions, energy, water, and garbage by 25 percent in our branch offices, businesses, warehouses, and on the part of our suppliers.

Over and above this, we will fully compensate for our worldwide CO_2 emissions through externally certified projects in other countries, with emphasis on Africa.

Implementation of paperless offices through a reduction of paper use by 75 percent, and support of reforestation projects to balance the remaining usage.

Introduction of the PUMA Sustainability Index (S-Index) as the measure for sustainability of each of our products, and for communication with our customers and consumers.

Production of 50 percent of all international collections in accordance with our PUMA S-Index by 2015, using sustainable materials such as organic-cotton, "Cotton

Made in Africa," or recycled polyester in the product lines in an environmentally friendly manner.

Full rollout of an innovative packaging and distribution concept for our products that will reduce the use of paper for shoeboxes in the future by 65 percent and CO_2 emissions to ten thousand metric tons per year. All remaining packaging materials should be fully sustainable by the year 2015. In addition, our textile collections will be packaged in sustainable material in the future, replacing the traditional synthetic polythene bags. In this way, 720 metric tons of synthetic bags will be saved each year, which is equivalent to a saving of twenty-nine million plastic bags. This in turn is the equivalent of a surface of one thousand football fields. Moreover, PUMA shirts will be folded one more time in order to decrease the packaging size and further reduce CO_2 emissions and transport costs. By using biodegradable bags made of cornstarch in place of shopping bags of plastic and paper in PUMA shops, we will save a further 192 metric tons of plastic and 293 tons of paper in the future. In addition we are endeavoring to make a positive contribution to society and promote peace as well as improving the social conditions of workers in the factories of our suppliers.

In brief: we are seeing to it that extensive actions follow our words, and we are taking a number of concrete steps so that our mission will increasingly become a reality. And yet, a lot more will need to be done to reduce our unsustainable ways and become more sustainable as a business.

ANSELM GRÜN: At Münsterschwarzach Abbey, it is important to me in a very concrete sense to ensure jobs for the long term so that there are no sudden fluctuations. Of course there are developments that lead to the need to close down certain areas, but then we must also see whether we can offer positions somewhere else. Rapid alternations between employment and layoffs are too expensive in the long run. Even the politics of staffing is all about sustainability.

Where the subject of sustainability is concerned, we don't have to invent things from the beginning like a business: we definitely have a clear competitive advantage in that regard. The monastery doesn't live just from the products it sells, but also from its organization, which is economical and sustainable and has little wasted energy. We have reduced bureaucracy in our administration and in the administration of our factories to a minimum.

A large share of the products that our workshops produce—furniture, electrical installations, whitewashing, welding, and so on—are not sold on the open market, but are designated purely for internal use. And we have made the decision in the abbey that we will not always ask for the cheapest offers of firms in the vicinity, but will deliberately accept a higher price if it means we can do business sustainably. Of course our workshops try to improve the cost structure, and we try to compare how much higher the costs of sustainable products are versus cheaper products. There must be a healthy relationship between the two. So we cannot arbitrarily say that sustainable products simply cost more. We need an appropriate relationship between better quality and higher costs.

Books make up a large part of our product offering, and this aspect of our business is primarily concerned with the ideas that we want to communicate to people. That is a matter of speaking a language that is nonjudgmental; and of touching people's hearts with our language, communicating the hope that life is worthwhile and can be successful.

With the other products that we sell—goods from our butcher, bakery, print shop, goldsmith, and bookstore—we have noticed that people don't look only at the price but also at the quality of the products. In this respect a monastery today definitely has an image advantage. People trust absolutely that everything we make has been sustainably produced and is of good quality. Of course good quality and sustainability of products must stand in a healthy relation to the price, but with us the customer pays an appropriate price, not an exaggerated one.

JOCHEN ZEITZ: You say that the customers are paying an appropriate price. I agree with this, and also think that we shouldn't underestimate consumers. Many of them have finally started to buy with greater awareness. Each time we stand at the checkout counter, we have the chance to decide which product and which brand we will purchase—within the range of what we can afford, that is. We can exert our influence by simply ceasing to buy products that pollute the environment and create excessive waste, for example.

If we are creative as companies and brands, we will also find ways to inform our consumers and link up with them, just as we must better inform ourselves in order to sharpen our own awareness of environmentally friendly businesses. Companies still have a lot to learn and a lot to do in this regard. We must become partners who bring their users along on the journey.

Furthermore, we companies are the ones who have instilled a certain kind of consumer behavior into our consumers. For this reason it is our responsibility to change our business practices and explain them more openly to the consumer in readily understandable language, instead of reproaching consumers for not being ready to pay a higher price for sustainability. As suppliers, we must change our ideas and as consumers, we must reprogram ourselves in the way we eat, drink, dress ourselves, and live.

CHAPTER 9

STRENGTHS AND WEAKNESSES

WITH AN INTRODUCTION BY
ANSELM GRÜN

As we strive to realize ethical ideals and bring about sustainability in our businesses, we constantly come up against our own mistakes and weaknesses when putting these ideas into practice. We are never unequivocally strong, yet we have been instructed to shape the world and form it in accordance with God's will, in spite of (or just because of) our weaknesses.

We can read about the topic of strength and weakness in the Bible, where Jesus relates the parable of the talents (Matthew 25:14–30). A man about to leave on a long trip calls in his three servants. He entrusts part of his fortune to them—a different amount to each one according to his ability (as the man sees it) to handle it. The first servant receives five silver coins, the second two, and the third just one. While the man is traveling, the first servant begins to do business with the money and doubles the amount that was entrusted to him. The second servant does the same, and he too earns a further two talents. The third servant is fearful of his master's harshness and buries his talent in the garden. When the man returns from his trip, he asks his servants what they have done with his money. The first two report their successes, and the man confers even greater duties on them, because he is not only satisfied with how they managed the talents, but believes them capable of further responsibility as well. Only the third servant finds no favor. The single coin that he dug up again is taken away from him and he is repudiated by his master.

Talents are abilities, strengths that we have received from God and which we ought to apply and develop in our lives. In the preceding parable, the first two servants get back the coins that the master had placed in their hands earlier. When you live your strengths, you become stronger and your powers become a blessing to others. The third servant is burying his coin and his potential talent, however. He is afraid of making a mistake and is afraid of his master, who could discover his weakness. Yet this third servant (with whom we instinctively sympathize, because he didn't get a share) is punished further. He is thrown into the "darkness, where there is howling and gnashing of teeth." With this parable, Jesus wants to say, "When you live with a safety-conscious attitude, when you hide away your talents because you are afraid of making mistakes, you will end up in the darkness of your unlived life. And when—purely out of fear—you seek to control everything, your life will go out of control and you will gnash your teeth at night." That is absolutely to be taken literally: I know several people who gnash their teeth at night. They want to control everything, even at night, including everything that turns up in their subconscious. They want to repress or suppress all this, but that isn't good either for the soul or for the teeth.

The person who has to marshal all his energies during his entire life to conceal his weakness is overtaxing himself; but when you answer for your weaknesses, you will find people to help you offset them. Then you can develop your strengths in friendship or cooperation with these people, and can strengthen others as well.

Every person has strengths and weaknesses. It is part of human maturity to be aware of this and acknowledge your qualities. There are people who constantly denigrate themselves and have no self-confidence, although they have capabilities. There are others who do not own up to their weaknesses and try to conceal them or cover them up. They live in fear that others could discover their faults. When they make a mistake, they cover this up and shift the blame to others, using considerable energy to keep their weaknesses secret.

This kind of behavior on the part of people in positions of leadership has major repercussions reaching beyond their personal spheres. When they cannot admit their weaknesses, these individuals take on too much. They make decisions for which they lack the necessary authority and act as if their instructions are the only correct ones. They won't let themselves be challenged, and hide their weaknesses behind exaggerated self-assurance and authority, which they outwardly project. But it is precisely these decisions made from a position of weakness that often have disastrous effects at the company level and on individuals' work within the company as well.

We ought to accept our strengths thankfully. They were given to us and are not our doing, but we have received them as a gift, so they become our duty as well: the duty of making a contribution with our strengths. This can be enjoyable for us and can become a blessing for others. The individual who hides his strengths all the time or excuses himself on account of them is restricting himself. Many people do not develop their strengths because they are afraid that others might envy them. But it is not very helpful when, for instance, the strong employees in a firm let themselves be held back by the envy of the weaker ones. This results in paralysis and increasing stagnation.

Admitting our faults is equally important, and the person who does this is strong rather than weak. In many firms there is a dominant climate in which no one dares to concede his weaknesses, because this would mean exposing himself or being ostracized. This kind of company culture is not beneficial.

135

HOW MANAGERS CAN TURN WEAKNESSES INTO STRENGTHS

When you answer for your weaknesses, you are recognizing your own abilities and limitations, and only someone who stands by his limitations will be able to overcome them. That is very important for managers, because the employee who acknowledges his weaknesses as well as his strengths encourages his coworkers to do the same. When you know the strengths and the weaknesses of every individual, you can employ them to best advantage.

A weakness may actually be a strength sometimes. It is a good sign when an executive manager of a company knows exactly where her strengths and weaknesses lie. Then she does not need to hide those weaknesses; instead, she can entrust an employee with a task she finds difficult. This serves two purposes: the employee learns from his superior to trust in his own competence, and the manager avoids overburdening herself.

Ideally, admitting weaknesses should help to alleviate a manager's difficulties in cases of conflict management and resolution. These problems can be acknowledged openly, and the manager can then consider how to reach a solution. She can decide who should be invited for discussion of the problem, and who has the necessary competence and mental independence to react to a heated situation with intelligence and careful reflection. By dealing with the matter in this way, the manager avoids suppressing the conflict or sidestepping it. This is tantamount to admitting: "I don't have to be able to do everything myself. When I am aware of my weaknesses, I seek out coworkers who are strong in the area where I am weak. That doesn't mean that I am subordinate to them; rather that I trust them to use their strengths to the benefit of the firm. In other words, I apportion work in such a way that the weak and strong stimulate each other instead of being mutually obstructive."

Saint Benedict expected to have weak as well as strong individuals in his community and decreed that the abbot should deal intelligently with this situation. Some managers only support the strong individuals, leaving the weak alone; or they may dismiss everyone who shows weakness. But this creates a climate in which everybody is afraid of being the next one to break under pressure. Such an atmosphere of fear doesn't support the strong, nor does it encourage the weak. There are also superiors who only concern themselves with the weak employees, and constantly appeal to the strong ones to be considerate of the weak. This is well intended, yet it often holds back the strong employees. All employees are kept at a lower level so that no one will stand out. That is not beneficial for either a company or its employees.

In his Rule, Saint Benedict orders the abbot to organize everything so that "the strong may have something to strive after, and the weak may not fall back in dismay" (Regula Benedicti 64:19). For Benedict this is the virtue of "discretion," the gift of distinguishing. The abbot should look precisely at what each individual needs; he must handle the strong differently from the weak and not overlook disparities between them. The abbot should challenge the strong, but not at the expense of the weak. He should not discourage the weak ones but help them, though not at the expense of strong individuals; rather, both sides must be supported. The abbot is instructed to create a climate in which the strong will be challenged to regularly contribute their strengths and thus bring the community forward. The weak should not desert the community, but use their power to the benefit of the whole.

The monastery's management of its monks is an important issue for Benedict. A monastery that reduces its complement of strong members cannot be self-sufficient in the long term, because it will be constantly preoccupied with itself. A monastery that overlooks the weaker monks will become debased at some point, because it has distanced itself from Christian principles.

For these reasons, it is important to give careful attention to the selection of young Brothers, maintaining a balance of weak and strong individuals to benefit both types.

When strong and weak individuals interact well, this is a boon for the community. A community shows true strength when it deals with its weak members much like treating the sick. But a company limits its own growth when it holds back strong individuals simply because the administrators are afraid those employees could become stronger than they are. Restraining employees in this way also uses up much energy and working capacity. The true art of leadership consists in supporting and challenging the strong, without discouraging the weak.

DIALOGUE: MANAGER AND MONK

JOCHEN ZEITZ: For some time, the personal weaknesses of managers as well as monks have been intensely observed and widely discussed in public. The Catholic Church is losing adherents and credibility on account of the abuse scandal. The business world has its own major crises with the global financial crisis and the shakeup of the Euro zone. In both worlds, men are being held up to ridicule because they were judged to be greedy and to have acted immorally, violated laws, and harmed others.

These are not new phenomena. Over the centuries, administrators who regarded themselves as part of an elite caste—in the business world just as in other parts of society—have often gone astray and sometimes failed spectacularly as well. One of the greatest problems of the bankrupt American firm Enron was its overconfidence. When you look closely at this large company's collapse, you recognize that the central group of the executive committee was made up of many arrogant people. They regarded themselves as so successful that in their eyes the general laws of humanity and nature were no longer valid for them.

Of course, major economic problems and crises don't happen only because of the lapses of a few bankers and managers. It is usually a whole system that fails. Before the recent financial crisis, for instance, there was an entire lineup of people who strove for advantage and profits: homeowners who really could not afford a second or third real estate property, but were out for a quick jackpot by reselling; lenders who waved through too many applications and hoped that the bubble would never burst; and investors who put money into high-interest securities that they didn't understand.

Who is to blame, then? In the last resort, is it only the grasping banker, inventor of the obscure financial products which leading investor Warren Buffett later described as "weapons of mass destruction"? Making scapegoats of a few people means avoiding our own responsibility. This is why we all—bankers, managers, or consumers—must recognize our weaknesses and learn from them in order to avoid future problems.

Managers ought to try to guarantee that they themselves and their employees are acting correctly. We executives carry the responsibility for the failures and transgressions of our companies. We are well paid for this—sometimes too well, the critics feel. But don't the same rules apply to us as to other people? Can't mistakes creep in without our being considered malicious and being publicly held liable? Certainly those who make large and far-reaching errors at the expense of others must be held responsible for this; but don't humaneness and fairness put limits on the errors which can be made public and stigmatized?

139

The reason for an offense should be more important than the offender's position: short-sightedness or an oversight should be assessed quite differently than deliberate deception, reckless power grabs, or personal rapacity! Father Anselm, you would surely also cite Jesus with his words to the multitude who wanted to stone a woman: "Whoever is without sin, let him throw the first stone."

Just as Pope Benedict has called the Church's crisis the "crisis from within," we managers and bankers must look at the crisis in the finance and business world from the inside, drawing our own conclusions and tackling changes in the system logically and with determination. Addressing mistakes comes down to four things: the individuals involved must face up to their responsibilities and their personal weaknesses; the particular system must have rules and laws which help to avoid mistakes and prevent cover-ups; we must make distinctions between multiple mistakes; and the system itself must be reformed and evolve. The Church, society, and business ought to develop further in this direction.

ANSELM GRÜN: I have watched the scandals in the financial sector and the abuse cases in the Catholic Church with great dismay. It seems normal to me that bank managers might make mistakes, but the way they handled these mistake is sometimes quite startling. Some of them only looked after their own profit, with open eyes and tremendous greed, but they then assumed no responsibility for their errors. They washed their hands of the whole thing, and after their downfalls they took legal action against their deeply unprofitable businesses for the recovery of outstanding bonus payments. I find that brazen. Mistakes happen, but I can only maintain my dignity when I stand up for my mistakes and don't act as if I can do nothing about them.

Of course I have also observed that society denounced bank employees in general, although many or even most of them had nothing to do with these affairs. For this reason it is important to look at this closely and not allow behavior to be accepted when it lacks ethical principles and honesty.

As a monk and member of the Catholic Church, however, I must take on the scandals in my own ranks. It is shameful that the Church, which often makes great moral claims, has not dealt appropriately with priests who have abused children. Unfortunately, sexual abuses were often covered up. Respect for the institution of the Church was given priority over the suffering of the victims. Not until 2002 did the German bishops' conference set up new guidelines for the handling of sexual abuse. The Church is being reproached today with its conduct before 2002, and the uncovering of cases of sexual abuse from the last forty to fifty years has thrown the Church into a deep crisis. It is important that the Church confront this crisis so that it can become a purifying crisis; then the manner in which the Church deals with the problem could have a truly cleansing effect on society.

The early monks said that instead of judging others, we should regard their mistakes as a mirror in which we all see our own dark sides. The Church's crisis can be salutary for itself and society if everyone looks into the mirror being held up to us by the media in their reports about abuse cases. That applies to all missteps, however, even those in the financial sector. If we see others only as scapegoats whom we must slaughter, nothing in society will change. Only when we are prepared to look into the mirror displaying our sins before our eyes will we mature in our development and thus find more humane relations.

141

JOCHEN ZEITZ: The monk as well as the manager lives within legal and cultural boundaries that change over the course of time, develop, are tested, and dissolve again. I think we must all find our own limits for working and living within that framework.

It is often forgotten that church and state have different mechanisms for responding to misguided desire. Religious legislation contains moral laws such as "turn the other cheek," "judge not" and "whoever is without sin, let him cast the first stone." This way of thinking is strikingly different from the secular laws in many countries. The latter are based on principles such as "fit the punishment to the crime," "an eye for an eye," and "equal treatment is the first principle of this nation." Consequently, the procedures and operative mechanisms in the Church's center of power cannot be compared with the mechanisms for reaching decisions and resolving conflicts that are used in modern corporations (among others). Corporate operations are based more on rational considerations, and so they may be more suitable for dealing with unusual situations and problems.

For this reason, those of us who consider ourselves committed to secular law have great difficulty understanding the alleged cover-up of abuse cases by a Church which (in accordance with its own culture) sets great store on forgiveness. A culture of forgiveness is easily misunderstood by a culture founded on secular justice. When a priest is "forgiven" and only receives a warning along with a second chance, then the outer world understandably has the impression, given the gravity of the offense, that he has not been punished appropriately. And this gives rise to the idea that there has been an injustice.

I fully endorse this line of thinking. In fact, I am of the opinion that hesitation or even lethargy (and in many cases the mentality of keeping quiet or covering up) are never acceptable under any circumstances if you want to tackle and solve questions and problems in a morally appropriate way, according to the rules. But I think that we must also try to understand what is happening and only then make up our minds, without sweeping condemnation from the start. This type of question is difficult to understand without a context of cultural transposition and moral development. Each outsider must learn to better understand the insider.

Just as we managers learn from our mistakes and must constantly improve our business methods, so most responsible individuals in the Church are surely ready to refine part of their archaic systems and methods, and submit to secular rules and laws in serious cases. The latest findings should be taken into account by establishing appropriate practical procedures and an institutional authority to handle abuse cases; or by improving selection of priests and having better monitoring of the priesthood, using modern psychoanalytical methods. I hope that in the future the Church will not only act quickly but will also take better preventive measures to minimize the danger of abusive behavior toward other people.

It is the experts' job to find the right answers in each of their specialties. However, this does not mean that companies have not had similar problems in the past and don't still have them. We only need to think of discrimination against minorities and the abuse of women—problems which led to stringent laws in many countries, particularly in the United States, although problems persisted then, and still exist in the world. This is in addition to the excesses that just became clear in the recent financial crisis and have cost many their livelihoods.

ANSELM GRÜN: Churches and business need the courage—and the humility—to look truth in the eye. The Latin word for humility, *humilitas,* comes from *humus,* meaning "earth, soil." It means the courage to accept one's own humanity, one's attachment to the earth: then we will be standing with both feet on the ground and will not lift away from it. There are managers who have too high an opinion of themselves. Observations such as "the others are all less well-off, they have no idea" are always a sign of this self-overvaluing. Hubris causes blindness: you refuse to look at your own reality and that of a company. You pretend something because you cannot put up with the truth. As a result, you flee from your own smallness into delusions of grandeur. The examples mentioned above show where that leads.

For executives, humility means being thoroughly acquainted with yourself, including your negative side and your weaknesses. Management personnel should not excuse themselves for their weaknesses, but accept them and be thankful at the same time for the strengths that God has also given. The company itself also needs humility. Sometimes the conviction takes hold in a company that it is the best company, and that other firms are to be scorned. When I devalue others, that is always an indication that I am afraid of being worthless myself. The person who knows his own value does not have to exalt himself above others.

Humility, then, means a realistic assessment of myself and a realistic evaluation of the company. We should be thankful for good cooperation, and humility will prevent us from rising above others. Even when a company is doing well, an exterior development can endanger its future overnight; or an unpredictable conflict may break out, and suddenly even a firm that has been praised to heaven is confronted with its own truth and weakness. When those in positions of responsibility in a company are excessively boastful, they must be careful that their fine words do not catch up with them. And when I am boastful on my own behalf, I will certainly be caught out by my weaknesses at some point. Humility is connected to courage—the courage to stand by yourself; the courage to step down into your own humanity and earthiness; the courage to remain with both feet planted on the ground, instead of elevating yourself above others.

JOCHEN ZEITZ: I am not certain whether those in control of a company generally need more humility. But managers and administrators ought to check their own conduct and attitudes constantly through critical self-observation. Managers should always be aware that their own prosperity is also dependent on the support and contributions of others. Instead of calling upon company leaders to show more humility, perhaps everybody should make an effort to show more humaneness. Every individual has his contribution to make to a better world, and can accomplish this. But the business world and its executives have to play a special role in this, for nothing else is so high-powered—either in the positive sense of steering in the right direction, or in the negative sense of putting themselves above important rules and principles and pursuing their own advantage in defiance of these.

ANSELM GRÜN: When money is the focus of attention, rather than God, then in my opinion a human being's conscience loses its determining power. When someone is only after money, he becomes irresponsible and no longer has any scruples. *Scruple* originally meant the little pointed

145

stone that stands for the pangs of conscience and painful doubt that push the individual to live in accordance with his truth and comply with the right order of values. The financial crisis has uncovered the unscrupulousness of many people. We have had painful experience of what can happen when people who handle money no longer have a conscience, and when they are no longer really aware of what they are doing.

CHAPTER 10

RESPONSIBILITY

WITH AN INTRODUCTION BY
JOCHEN ZEITZ

In many older cultures, a Zen master or shaman would use a puzzle or a story to help people seeking their enlightenment. Socrates, Plato, and Aristotle also used images, just like the wise masters and teachers in many Eastern cultures.

Let us imagine that we are sitting around the campfire of such a master, who asks the following riddle: "Three gardeners were tending a large garden. The first one worked all the time and didn't leave his part of the garden until all the weeds were removed and the entire harvest was brought in. The second gardener did not work as many hours, but when the garden needed his attention because the grain was ripe or a drought threatened, he worked even harder than the first gardener. The third gardener decided that he needed breaks and time for self-contemplation, to examine his vocation and his life's direction; so he left the garden now and then. Which gardener truly showed a sense of responsibility?"

Presumably we would reply, "The first gardener obviously shows the greatest sense of responsibility, because he works the most." Or, "It's quite clear that it is the second gardener; he is the sort we need for garden care. He knows that he has to work hard when it matters." Which one of us would choose the third gardener, who apparently abandons the garden and doesn't assume his responsibility?

The master who gave us this riddle directs our thinking in a different direction: "I would answer that all three have demonstrated a true sense of responsibility. We need all of them, and not just for a well-tended garden. Responsibility isn't only about the task that is waiting to be done. Sometimes we don't listen to our inner voice, which advises us from a higher perspective to carry out the gardening tasks in a different way. The person who hears this voice might decide to give up what he has been doing routinely all year. Given some distance, he will recognize his own mistakes and identify new ways to work more effectively in the future. This is how he can become a better gardener. Sometimes it is necessary to make your way to a new level in order to hear this inner voice. It leads to a new vision and along a new path to a new garden."

Our master continues: "Responsibility is not only the duty of being answerable to one's superiors and family. There is also a responsibility to something much greater: to God, to the higher self, and to the earth. So let us not be too severe with the third gardener, who may learn during his pauses how he can work better, if not harder, or who might take over another garden where better field crops grow. We should not scorn the second gardener just because he does not work all the time. He has learned to act in harmony with life cycles. Just like nature, he saves energy when the seed is resting dormant in the earth. He prepares himself to work twice as hard when the harvest must be brought in quickly before frost sets in. Our ancestors knew exactly how they had to work along with the cycles of the sun's energy, and they were outstanding gardeners because they understood nature's rhythm and worked in accordance with it. But that doesn't mean that the first gardener is superficial or less important. His dedication and devotion to the garden is priceless, and in a time of need there is always at least one trustworthy gardener standing ready. Even when there is apparently no harvest to bring in, he prepares himself all the same for the next cycle and improves the fences. If the second gardener represents natural balance and the third gardener represents wisdom, then the first one stands for stability. He is trustworthy and guarantees that soil and vegetation are always well looked after. All three gardeners are needed in life, and all three show a real sense of responsibility."

At this point, the master finishes, and the moral of what is known as The Parable of the Garden is: All of them are called. And each one is capable of taking on responsibility.

THE RESPONSIBILITY TO ACT

Let us consider for a moment the thinking of the philosopher Jean-Paul Sartre and his conception of responsibility. Sartre would say that Man is not only responsible for his deeds but also for his failures to act. For example, while I am writing or you are reading, hunger and poverty and environmental destruction are advancing in many parts of the world. According to Sartre, you and I are responsible for this. Of course we would protest against this: after all we do not know enough about what is happening in distant parts of the world. Besides, we could hardly do anything to change the tragic circumstances there. Sartre would counter that you and I have decided to remain uninformed. I, for example, am deciding just now to write these words instead of becoming engaged and doing something about hunger and poverty. When all is said and done, I could organize a fundraising drive or draw attention to the situation using my contacts. But I decide to ignore this possibility, and also decided not to give anything to the man who just rang my doorbell, collecting money for the Children's Aid

149

Foundation to benefit neglected and abused children. I always have responsibility for what I am doing, and also for the things that I prefer to ignore or leave undone.

We have a responsibility or—to express this in a way that may be more motivating—we have a chance to free ourselves from a "programmed" life. Everyone can see for himself what has to be done, instead of blindly maintaining the status quo or following the group like a pack of lemmings. This doesn't mean questioning every action, however small, such as why we usually take the same route when jogging, habitually write with the right hand, or always reason in the same way. It has to do instead with the larger question of what we want to do with our lives. If we don't ask this and our existence is routine, as the sociologist Max Weber called it, then are we really aware of responsibility? Are we taking into consideration options that free up our thoughts or have meaning for our existence?

It is against this background that the American philosopher Lorraine Code speaks about "epistemic responsibility"— responsibility related to the theory of knowledge—in her book of the same name.[1] She posits the thesis that man has a duty to think, and that this is meaningful in a wider context. For example, if I travel from North America to England, I am responsible for knowing that I must drive on the left side of the street. If I build an atomic power station, I assume responsibility for knowing what a core meltdown in this facility would mean for the surrounding area.

Managers confront this epistemic responsibility in many ways. For instance, in the PUMA production line, when we use cotton that was grown exclusively for this purpose, then there is a connection between me and the manner of growing and harvesting that cotton. So I am partially responsible for whether pesticides, children, or underpaid pickers are used. When I use leather from Brazilian cows raised in certain regions, I am co-responsible for the destruction of the rainforests that are cleared for cattle farming.

150

PERSONAL RESPONSIBILITY

Where does my responsibility begin, and where does it end? Am I acting responsibly when I pay only a minimum wage or economize in my reliance on environmentally friendly materials and suppliers? Or when I slow down reforms in a production run to achieve markedly higher profits? Isn't it the case that my responsibility grows in proportion to my awareness of the results of my actions?

If you think about the Zen masters and philosophers, then it becomes clear that responsibility doesn't just mean carrying out certain duties. Instead, it means knowing what duties there are to be carried out and with whom, what the results can be, and whether the right person for this job is competent. This means that I bear an individual, social, and global responsibility and don't just play the part of the first or second gardener.

For those who carry out managerial duties, it is not always simple to become aware of this greater responsibility. When I took over the care of the PUMA garden, if I can call it that, there were many weeds in it and many quarreling gardeners. Our market presence had been extremely weak for some time already. In his book *The PUMA Story*, Rolf-Herbert Peters tellingly sums up the plight of our brand in the mid-1980s. Peters writes that he was completely surprised when he saw the PUMA logo (on television) on Boris Becker's tennis racket. His reaction at that time was, "PUMA: does it still exist?" After this downfall and years of heavy losses, the company was endangered when I arrived. My only responsibilities appeared to consist of watering the garden and making it fruitful again.

My sense of responsibility has broadened over the years. In the beginning it took in my own person and my family; then came the workplace and my career. Today I feel at least co-responsible for a much larger circle: my community and the earth on which we live. Beyond this is a still larger responsibility, possibly the largest

151

responsibility which a human being can have: the responsibility to God or to a superior Power.

Today I try to do everything in my power to make up for omissions. I am deeply thankful to all those who saw—long before me—the necessity of a new vision and resolute action. Also to those who today, every day, hear their own wake-up call to assume responsibility for the community and the environment. We are all being challenged, for only together can we bring humankind and nature back into an evolutionary and natural equilibrium.

TOPPLING THE NEXT BERLIN WALL

Just as there was a Berlin Wall, which many of us experienced and which eventually fell, there are still walls within each of us that hold back global awareness and the global responsibility for our planet that must be torn down and can be cleared away. There are walls made of prejudices, short-sightedness, regional bias, and intellectual obstinacy, and global responsibility begins with awareness of these walls. It also begins with the idea of regarding oneself as a citizen of the world who lives together with others in a common and endangered living space. Fear of major responsibility is widespread, for various reasons, but in the course of history many walls erected by humans have been torn down: slavery, Apartheid, and the Berlin Wall have fallen. We should try to tear down the walls within ourselves, too.

It is a fallacy to assume that global responsibility is a virtually insoluble, Herculean task. This perspective corresponds to that of the first gardener, who sees himself continuously cultivating his garden without interruption around the clock. Behind the idea that such a great responsibility cannot be shouldered is the awareness that responsibility always means more and never less.

Al Gore's Oscar-winning documentary *An Inconvenient Truth* conveys the message that we have an enormous problem to resolve. But the film contains a further important finding: changes in personal thinking are both necessary and possible. In a moment of self-revelation, the former American vice president talks in the film about how his family lived from traditional tobacco farming in Carthage, Tennessee, where he grew up. He relates how his sister became ill with lung cancer and eventually died from it. Gore, who loved his sister very much, describes the despair of his family after her death. The most tragic thing was the realization that every member of the family had contributed in a certain sense to lung cancer or had even caused it, for without the cultivation and sale of tobacco, Al Gore's sister would not have been exposed to the damaging effects of the plant. After the family recognized the tragic irony of their situation, they stopped growing tobacco, although it had become their chief source of income.

Such a realization shows the deeper significance of the film: personal change is possible—and without it there will be no true solution for major problems. Gore's implication in the film is: if I can do this, we can, too. To put it another way: when Al Gore and his family stopped growing tobacco, their action corresponded to the third gardener in our parable. We, too, can make changes. Al Gore's intimate story also shows that deep-reaching personal change must precede global change. The end is the beginning.

A large part of our responsibility does not consist in shouldering an unbearable weight, but rather in throwing off an unhealthy burden. It isn't a question of hoisting up a dumbbell that gets heavier and heavier; rather, it is about removing the causes of problems.

Responsibility can also involve fulfillment and joy. For this reason I have always greeted it and have not tried to avoid it. Frequently, responsibility leads us to new adventures in which we meet admirable people of integrity who are also making a contribution and want to change something. In my life, more responsibility has meant more

153

travel and culture, friendships, and tremendous moments in sport rather than a life full of rigid, monotonous drudgery. That is a great happiness, too! It is as if my life rewarded me from the time I stopped working against nature and decided to become a friend of life.

For the new era of global sustainability really to be effective, we must close the old chapter of our inadequate responsibility and recognize our own contribution to the state of the Planet, and be accountable.

DIALOGUE: MANAGER AND MONK

ANSELM GRÜN: In our day-to-day management, we are constantly confronted with the question of what the protection of the environment is worth. That often starts on a small scale, for example with trees that stand in a front garden or close to a house. When we renovate a building, it is often practical, of course, to fell the trees which are standing too close, so that we have more room for the machinery and can work more efficiently. Yet we often make a very conscious decision to leave the trees standing, especially when they are healthy older trees. The director of an institution for those with dementia, which is located in an old villa, once told me that she had deliberately retained the old stock of trees during renovations, but that led to her having to pay the cost of a tall crane which could bring prefabricated units over the old trees and into the building.

Another example: we maintain a water turbine in the monastery with which we obtain around 7 percent of our power. To keep the turbine running, we have to repeatedly clean and maintain the stream. These costs are not recovered by the power output, but we undertake this work gladly because when we do this, we are also caring for nature and keeping nature in good condition. The beauty of nature and the brook with its avenue, a living space for many songbirds, are worth the expense to us. With respect to nature, not all decisions can be made from a strictly monetary viewpoint. However, it is certainly sensible to calculate the costs of preserving nature, so that we can make these decisions in an informed way.

JOCHEN ZEITZ: There are three basic aspects of the economy which we must consider: what it takes, what it produces, and what it wastes. All three are closely interconnected. But companies must change this ineffective traditional behavior responsibly and consistently, and convert to sustainable management. For these reasons, sustainability is fixed in our vision, mission, and positioning at PUMA, as mentioned previously, which means that it is anchored in our company and brand approach. This allows for sustainable shareholder value enhancement and sustainable growth as well. This inevitably involves capital expenditure as well.

ANSELM GRÜN: It will be a task for the future to develop technologies which are designed right from the beginning toward the goal of careful treatment of the environment. But technology doesn't always have the right attitude to use its innovations in a good way. The most environmentally friendly technology will not help if Man is influenced by fearful behavior patterns, and uses that technology as an instrument of control instead of support. Whether technology becomes a blessing or not depends on the way it is used. Let us take the computer as an example: we save considerable paper by writing e-mails and contribute to the protection of the environment when we do this. But this advantage is negated when we use e-mails as an

155

instrument of domination, constantly bombarding our employees with reports and demanding immediate replies from them. I know employees who spend a large part of their time answering senseless e-mails from the boss, just so the boss will feel that everything is under control.

The advantages of technology are annulled when our businesses are dominated by fear. When that happens, we need records for everything, and the records must be written out, printed on paper, and documented in file folders. Fear not only swallows up human energy, but eventually damages the environment as well. Nature is characterized by self-confidence and independence: plants grow by themselves. When we control them, we destroy them in the middle of their growth. We sometimes believe that all human activities have to be monitored and documented, yet this just inhibits healthy and natural growth and wastes energy.

JOCHEN ZEITZ: Supervision limits the responsibility of every individual, but as human beings we cannot entirely do without it. Every person can and must have freedom in his work as in his life as a whole, in order to be able to assume responsibility. Every individual needs responsibility, for without it he loses interest and joy in his activities. We say that a person "takes on" responsibility. When we have the feeling that we can assume still more responsibility, then in my opinion we will find the means and ways to do this.

ANSELM GRÜN: As an executive manager, however, you must also grant this responsibility to your employees. Often that is not so easy. One of my strengths is having confidence in my employees. But every strength always has a downside, too. Mine is that I sometimes demand too little and steer in the direction things are going. But in the thirty-four years that I have been Cellarer, I have learned to sometimes select employees more able to do those things that I do not do so well. In this way my weaknesses do not disturb the work in the community.

Taking on responsibility also means assuming responsibility for our own weaknesses. Even as a child, I constantly had new ideas that I tried to develop, alone or with my siblings, but I rarely had to battle resistance. I could easily fill my siblings with enthusiasm, so that they gladly went along with my suggestions. My strengths and weaknesses resulted from these experiences. My strength is that I work quickly and effectively, always have new ideas, and am constantly trying something out. My weakness is that it is difficult for me to tackle conflicts and follow through against the resistance of employees or other Brothers. Now I have learned to handle conflict better and also to fight for what is important to me; yet I recognize the tendency in myself to avoid unpleasantness and perhaps to wait it out.

JOCHEN ZEITZ: I have learned over time to accept the fact that as a human being, I have weaknesses that I must live with. For a long time, I had weaknesses so deeply buried inside me that I managed to function and work without knowledge of them. I have learned from this—and am still continuing to learn—to be watchful and recognize my weaknesses. When I make myself aware of them, then it is more difficult or impossible for them to run rampant in secrecy and thwart my intentions and plans.

In 2010, I asked an independent auditor to assess my achievements in relation to that of my colleagues. I wanted to guarantee in this way that I would be aware of all weaknesses that perhaps were still hidden from my view. Like the old Serenity Prayer that advises composure,

I try "to change the things I can change and accept the things I cannot change." I have aimed for perfection and additional responsibility so often in my career that I have sometimes forgotten to be satisfied or thankful when I am successful. As soon as I reached a goal, I was already searching for a dark cloud on the horizon and asking myself what else could go wrong! Today I recognize that by striving for success with ever-greater responsibility, I have sometimes made it difficult for the people around me.

ANSELM GRÜN: I observe in myself, as one example, that I am dependent on the atmosphere around me, so I often let my mood be dampened by outside influences. Then it is a spiritual challenge to meditate myself away from these negative feelings, and to blow cleansing breath into the anger. Or I pray the Jesus Prayer into these negative feelings. The atmosphere that I spread around me is my responsibility; I don't want to set up a high ideal which I cannot reach.

Saint Benedict challenges the Cellarer to watch his own soul all the time. The soul often shows me my negative feelings; no one can get around them. But watching the soul also means watching these negative feelings and cleansing them through meditation. If that doesn't work, I have to at least distance myself from those feelings for the duration of my working time. When I cannot clear them up at a particular moment, then I say to myself: "Now I won't take these feelings along to the meetings. I will leave them outside." Afterwards I take time to look more closely at them and clarify them. In this way an atmosphere emerges where something can grow and bloom. Otherwise the dark cloud of my unresolved feelings settles on the whole department and contaminates everything.

CHAPTER 11

AWARENESS

WITH AN INTRODUCTION BY
ANSELM GRÜN

The word *consciousness* means that I am aware of my own existence, my being. We monks see this differently from our traditional perspective: we believe that we change our being through our consciousness. From their earliest days, religious orders accepted the conviction that reading the Bible determined one's view of things. And when we *see* things differently, they *become* different for us, too. Our consciousness, developed through contact with the Bible and through prayer and meditation, transforms the world.

Martin Buber has passed along wonderful Hasidic stories about pious rabbis who often presented their teachings in a humorous way. Rabbi Chanoch, for example, related the following story:

> Once upon a time there was a fool who was so foolish that he was called Golem. When he got up in the morning, it was always so difficult for him to get his clothing together that when he thought about this in the evening, he was almost afraid to go to sleep. One evening he finally took heart, picked up a pencil and a piece of paper, and wrote down where he put each item. In the morning he cheerily pulled out the scrap of paper and read: "cap: here it

is," and he put it on. "Trousers: there they lie," and he pulled them on—and so on, until he had all his clothes on. "Yes, but where am I, then?" he asked himself with alarm. "What about me?" However he searched and looked around, it was in vain: he couldn't find himself. And that is the way things are with us.[1]

The rabbi's story applies to many people. They know what they ought to wear, how they should behave outwardly, how to work, and how to present themselves to others. They are not conscious of themselves and have no awareness of themselves, and so they also live without awareness in the world. They do not truly perceive themselves, others, or the world itself. They simply live from day to day.

Many executive managers, too, are so totally wrapped up in their daily business that they hardly know who they really are. However, if they do not perceive themselves, they will also not notice their employees as distinct people. They will regard them merely as human capital or as cogs in the wheels of machinery, but won't see their special character as human beings. Because they have no relationship to their own selves, these managers also cannot form a real relationship to others or the company. The person who is not aware of herself will also fail to make contact with what matters to others.

Administrators like to give the impression that they are correct and cool-headed, but that leads to the suppression of their negative aspects. Then they use too much energy bottling up those qualities in themselves which they deny. A woman once said to me, for instance, that she could not tolerate silence because it gave her the feeling that a volcano was going to blow up inside her. When you live with such an image, you need considerable energy to "keep the lid on the volcano," and then that energy is not available for your work. Yet you still live in fear that the seal will give way and the volcano will explode sometime. Living consciously means being aware of your negative aspects, but that doesn't mean acting them out. Instead, they must be integrated into your current life concept.

Consider the case of a boss who shows only one side of himself to his employees. When he is anxious for his staff to do their best, he may slide into contradictory behavior if they disappoint him. He will then act out his aggressions and direct animosity at them, because he blames them for his disappointment. It is important that he integrate these aggressions into his friendly relations with the employees. Aggressions control the circumstances of closeness and distance: when I am aggressive, this shows that I have not protected my limits, and that others have crossed my boundaries. This causes me to be emotionally confused, because the boundaries are blurred and everything is unclear. Gestalt theory refers to this as *confluent personalities*: I can no longer distinguish my feelings from those of my surroundings; in other words, I can no longer see the situation with clarity.

KNOWING YOURSELF—THE GOOD AND THE BAD

Consciousness or awareness, then, means first of all being aware and assured about your own self, knowing your own light and shadow sides, and accepting them. This self-awareness should not be confused with self-assurance, when someone supposedly knows that he can do something and shows great confidence on the outside. Behind such self-assurance there is often an individual who is not aware of himself, who doesn't know himself, but only behaves in this way on the outside. That is the opposite of self-assurance. The Greeks talk of *syneidesis* and the Romans speak of *conscientia*. These concepts mean "knowing with," a shared seeing. The concept of conscience grew out of this in Stoic philosophy and later in the Christian tradition. Actually the term means that I not only

161

know something but also am aware of knowing it—it is a collaborative knowledge, a conscious knowing. Conscience is the highest standard for an individual's decision making, even standing above the laws prescribed by society. Our conscience must develop first, however. It is our task to cleanse our conscience of our own moods and desires and the demands of our so-called "superego."

When someone is aware of her own self and has integrated her negative side, she can work to the advantage of a company. But if this is not the case, the company can be adversely affected. What applies to the individual also applies to groups. There are firms that seem to be very idealistic in their plans and what they want to achieve, but they have their negative aspects, too. A company may espouse the cause of ecology and treat nature gently, but its handling of the people in the business may not be in the same spirit; it may exploit its employees, for instance. Another company, which is vocal about Christian values, does not notice how un-Christian its language has become, how unfeelingly it passes judgment on its employees, or how much authority and pressure are exerted through its moralizing insistence on Christian values. It is also true for businesses that where there is light, there is shadow, too. This means that where idealism and company philosophy are close to becoming an ideology, there are bound to be problems of which the company is unaware.

These weaknesses can be recognized from the way in which a company talks about other businesses. We can always assume a downside when a firm is boastful on the outside, advocating high ideals and using grand words. There is a sister monastery of ours which is a case in point. This monastery announced that its community's slogan would be "We are a house of love." That sounds wonderful, yet an employee from this monastery said to me, "Since we've become a house of love, it has been getting colder and colder here." I don't want to name any particular companies, for then I would be in danger of judging others, but when I see noble images, I would like to jog the consciences of the responsible

162

parties, to see whether there is a hidden downside. A company that always wants to do the best will certainly make mistakes. The danger is that it will not admit these mistakes or will project them onto others. When someone rails against other people, he is trying to distract attention from his own weaknesses.

Where his religious orders were concerned, Benedict insisted on *stabilitas*, staying in the same place. The strength of this idea lies in the fact that a monastery works sustainably because it looks after its environment well. After all, people who want to continue living in a place have a personal interest in shaping their surroundings beautifully, to last for years to come. The negative side of this idea, however, is the rigidity and sometimes stolidity which are inherent in many monasteries. The mendicant orders are significantly more mobile, and are often closer to people. But even behind the ideal of poverty there are often hidden desires, unacknowledged but acted out nonetheless.

Every company has a dark side, and businesses as well as individuals need the Benedictine virtue of humility to become aware of these negative aspects. Jung insists that such "shadows" be integrated into the personality. Today we talk about *accepting* weaknesses instead and are more cautious about the notion of integrating those shadows.

It is a significant achievement for a company to become aware of its problems and accept them. It can then become more honest and conduct itself more modestly, including in dealings with other firms. The greater the awareness of company weaknesses, the clearer relations among employees will become, and there will be fewer hidden problems in the company's public philosophy. I am not entitled to identify the downside of the PUMA firm, for I know too little of the company. But regardless of the philosophy a company espouses, it is certainly wise to look into the question of weak areas, for this will help make the company philosophy clearer and more realistic. When images are too idealistic, I always detect strong shadows behind them.

Awareness has still another meaning, however. There is much talk today of ecological and social awareness, awareness of the solidarity of all mankind, and an all-embracing consciousness. Management has a duty to concern itself with the state of awareness or consciousness in the company, and to open employees' eyes so that they perceive the world as it is. This is a matter of looking at the global situation with intellectual clarity and making ourselves aware of how we can react to it appropriately.

It is our job, then, to portray the situation of our world unsparingly, and to create a feeling on the part of our fellow men for the interconnectedness of events in global affairs. We have the duty to sharpen our employees' awareness of their responsibility for the whole world. The more we bring about awareness of sustainability and ethically correct actions in the world, the more we will be able to change reality.

DIALOGUE: MANAGER AND MONK

JOCHEN ZEITZ: Like a monk, a manager must also broaden his awareness constantly and help his team to do the same. Awareness of business-related issues is just as important as an awareness of the personal spheres that concern and influence the company.

However, there are certain difficulties in connection with awareness of reality and the description of this reality in public, and I would like to touch on them here. I consider it sometimes difficult, for example, for a manager responsible for a company to portray his firm's current situation in a completely realistic and unsparingly truthful way: he cannot. In a publicly traded company, he can bring major problems upon himself if he discusses certain weaknesses. There are several reasons for this.

First of all, everyone expects nothing but success stories all the time. Yet the media can inflate a self-disclosure into a sensational story, if they are disappointed in the original information. Moreover, competition is tough, and a company's rivals can use an admission from that company to their advantage. A company's acknowledgment of its downside can lead to criticism and the loss of customers if the wrong, destructive channels unfairly exploit these weaknesses. Our society is structured so that competing institutions cannot speak willingly and openly about their shortcomings. In our culture, everyone is too quick to gossip, assign blame, and condemn.

ANSELM GRÜN: Like you, I do not believe that a firm ought to present its downside to the public. To me it is more an issue of knowing about our weaknesses; then our self-representations will be more realistic. Of course we will publicize our strengths, but in language that doesn't exaggerate and remains modest. I am always skeptical when somebody is boastful. I feel this way with spiritualist preachers, company representatives, and at lectures about new management models. When everything looks perfect, that always signals to me that the shadow side is being omitted.

We have an advantage as a monastery, because we are not usually under such intense public pressure as a corporation, nor do we have to compete as fiercely. As a result, we don't have to present ourselves to the outside world in an idealized way to attract attention. But the disadvantage of this is that we are only too happy to rest on the laurels of our past. We have difficulty coping with scandal, and we are certainly not as innovative as many modern firms. On the other hand, we can be happy that we are not under the kind of pressure that public companies endure, so we can continue with our work without interruption. Sometimes, however, we limp behind and do not make a great enough effort.

Let's look at the economic side: we have a management advisory board that deliberates about the future of our monastery. But because we don't have as much pressure to control costs as many other firms, we are in danger of continuing to manage as we have always done, without thinking in new ways about whether we can support ourselves as a company in the future as well. The management advisory board is aware that the abbey is going to have to adapt to living without the income from my books and lectures. Yet things are going well for us at the moment, and the Brothers do not yet feel the pressure to switch tracks to a different kind of management to guarantee the continued existence of the monastery and its projects. The advantage of being able to reflect in quiet is often outweighed by the disadvantage of failing to examine our management rigorously enough or explore new pathways.

JOCHEN ZEITZ: The director of a company must act quickly, and constantly examine himself. The business world is all about the survival of the strongest. Just as natural evolution intends that only those who adapt best should survive, so companies collapse when they don't keep pace with evolution and cannot adapt to new circumstances or develop themselves further.

Nature didn't need a "referee"—at least, not until the human species came into play. With our knowledge today, we can and must set down better rules for the economy that conform to society, the rules of nature, and the new knowledge which we have gained in this connection. Then the referee can act accordingly and intervene. Those who don't want to follow the new rules of the game must (after a warning) be shown first the yellow and then the red card. In the final analysis, the successful companies of the future will not only be the new, innovative, and fastest companies but also those able to reinvent themselves by acknowledging and accepting reality in conformity with the new ecological and social paradigm. The companies in this group will have the courage and inspiration to start a new game. Developing further or failing—isn't that a part of evolution theory, too?

ANSELM GRÜN: Of course it is; but the question is: how fast must everything go? Many firms squander a lot of energy on constant restructuring without really developing themselves further. They want to demonstrate their vitality to the outside world, yet they do not carry out change with inner peace of mind, wise intuition, or vision, but rather implement it in an agitated and unreflective rush. Rushing is a febrile condition, however, that indicates illness and not further development. Every firm, including monasteries, must change itself, but it is always a question of speed. Here, too, we can learn from nature, which changes and grows continually, but precisely at the speed that corresponds to its essence. Turning to the competitive situation, the only competition between monasteries has to do with the number of new entrants, but this is hardly a financial competition. Different monasteries serve different markets, and even their schools are not in competition with each other, because they are limited to regional catchment areas for their students.

On the other hand, our business operations such as printing, publishing and bookselling, the bakery, and the butcher shop are already in competition with other printers, presses, bookstores, and so forth. Here we have to be up to date and technically and managerially innovative, and we must identify which niches we can serve. If we don't take care of this, then operations will decline, and that could call into question the financial basis of our monastery.

In the monastery itself, we are also in a competition—a spiritual competition. Only monasteries living out a vital spirituality will be attractive for younger people over the long term. So it is always a question of whether we progress further spiritually or whether we stop, and whether we can give a suitable response to the questions of contemporary individuals. We monasteries are not going to woo people away from each other. But the impression that a monastery makes in the outside world will decide whether young people want to enter it or not. The existential question for us—namely, whether a monastery can continue to exist in the long term—depends on whether there are enough young men who want to join and who will carry things forward in a positive way. For this we don't need hangers-on but fellow Brothers who will assume responsibility and are able to lead.

JOCHEN ZEITZ: There is definitely no spiritual competition in businesses, nor any so-called spiritual awakening. Companies and managers wouldn't attempt to aim for a spiritual competition. In the last resort, it is the job of each individual person to handle his own spirituality and spiritual convictions in his private sphere. Besides, employees who already have their own beliefs might feel discriminated against in their own convictions if a company adopted a spiritual stance.

In questions of spirituality and religion, companies should show tolerance and freedom, and in this secular world, managers should not prescribe any religion in their corporate capacity, or model any religion in an emphatic manner. At the same time, I do not try to negate the positive influence of a spiritual presence. Spiritually oriented people who are professional and capable in their jobs can take on quite high positions in a company, without ever having to preach their beliefs. They can bring a balanced, positive, inspiring, and sometimes even healing mood to the company.

Aside from this, every company has its own special spirit. Even if no religious terminology is used within a firm, there is still an invisible spirit or attitude that propels a successful company, just as a monastery uses many visible business practices to remain financially self-sufficient.

ANSELM GRÜN: Executives in a multinational company certainly ought to be careful about favoring a religion. But generally speaking, a company should have a sense for religion, because religion has the job of broadening human consciousness and opening the horizons of thinking to God. When religion holds heaven open above mankind, it is making an important contribution toward humanizing society. For society, like every firm, has an absolutist tendency. It wants total control over Man and wants to judge only according to economic points of view, ranking all human activity according to financial categories. That is not good for humanity. Religion protects that which is sacred in Man and keeps this apart from the world. There is a divine space in each person that is not subject to worldly power. The individual can breathe there, and his soul takes flight. Only a winged soul can bestow wings on other people; and without the soul's wings, a company loses its impetus. It still functions, but it doesn't raise itself into the air to see everything from above in a different light.

169

One other last aspect is important for me: when I withdraw from work to meditate and pray, I become more creative. Often my best thoughts come to me during meditation. Leaving behind the obsession with work and its problems lets my thinking spread out and allows new ideas to surface in me. During meditation, I come in contact with the inner source of the Holy Spirit, always an inspiring source that gives me new ideas. Setting your work aside and immersing yourself in your own soul in prayer and meditation has an inspiring and motivating effect on your work, too.

JOCHEN ZEITZ: There are many different ways to broaden one's awareness, establish distance, and let oneself be inspired—both with and without direct belief in God. I myself grew up in a traditional Evangelical, engaged, and open-minded parental home with two older siblings. As a child and youth, belief in God was a fixed element of my life. However, during my university studies and up until a few years ago, belief played almost no part in my life anymore. It wasn't until a few years ago that I came into contact with the Christian religion again through my interest in psychology and philosophy, and later through my meetings with you, Father Anselm, and my one-week stay at Münsterschwarzach. Since then, my spirituality has been developing with growing strength, and so has my belief in a great, higher power and my personal conception of my life as part of the whole. Today I feel connected and close to all world religions, and I believe in the common roots of all of them.

As mentioned earlier, the outlook on life formulated by Buddha is particularly well suited to me. There is no final meaning or ultimate sense of life, just life itself. You speak of conscious being, Father Anselm. For me, this is how inner happiness grows out of being. Simply to be ourselves, to realize our enlightened being, which experiences life with its various ups and downs: that is the foundation of existence that brings fulfillment, quite independently of where our personal strengths and weaknesses may lie. Of course different religions and philosophical movements have different names for the concept of fulfillment. Whether they speak of "sustainable enlightenment," "goal-directed living," "maximized potential," "the greatest good," "devotion," or "a satisfied life in a small room," the central message is: *being* is worthwhile in itself—but not *being rich, being powerful,* or *being first.*

Eastern teachings say that the individual is supported by the river of life. As soon as we take on the responsibility to follow the Tao or life path—or, expressed in Western terms, to live a well-balanced life—many things become clearer and simpler. The result of this is more joy in life.

Father Anselm, we have spoken a good deal about God and money. I think that we can consider those two concepts together when we call on our conscience, the higher authority in our consciousness, to help us judge correctly.

ANSELM GRÜN: God and money belong together naturally. Money is the original sacrifice presented to God, the ritual payment owed to God. Our conscience shows us whether we are handling money properly—whether we are letting it take the place of God, or keeping God as our focal point, with money merely serving to regulate life well. You call the conscience the higher authority in our consciousness. From the meaning of the Greek word—*syneidesis,* or "knowing together"—conscience means the godly witness who guarantees that we conform to God and to our true essence.

171

God and conscience belong together, just as God and money do. We hear God's voice in our conscience. If the intrinsic connection between the three concepts of God, money, and conscience collapses, then money takes the place of God and money rules the world, becoming the maxim of human thoughts and deeds. Money becomes an idol and draws all human energies into itself. It becomes the only value that still has validity for human beings. But if humans regard money as the only value, and neglect the values which determine their humanity—those same values which Greek philosophy and Christian theology revealed as the expression of human dignity—then money will also be worthless. The financial crisis demonstrated this clearly: when everything that determines value in our lives is projected onto money, then our lives become worthless.

On the other hand, when people working in a company let themselves be inspired by religion, this stimulates their existence together. They do not judge fellow employees only by their accomplishments, but notice their personal radiance; and the radiance of an inspired person is more positive than that of a person who only pecks like a chicken at the grain on the floor. In antiquity, *grain pecker* was a derogatory term. The Stoic philosophers scolded Paul after his speech on the Areopagus with the question, "What does this grain picker (prattler) want?" (Acts 17:18) They meant that he would only pick up what was lying on the ground, but had no vision, no rousing idea.

Man needs the wings of religion, then, to see the bigger picture—and of course such a view into the distance includes a view of globalization and the future of the universe.

172

JOCHEN ZEITZ: All of us should keep looking beyond our usual parameters and think outside the box to recognize that "business as usual" belongs to the past. Then we will stop looking only at the microscopic world of our own company, and set up the "macroscope" to discern the complete, holistic picture.

Science teaches us that in the final analysis, everything is a connected whole, like the universe. In addition, most world religions teach that there is already oneness, and only our fractured human consciousness projects separations onto the planet. We human beings must broaden our perspective and try to understand our global, coalescent world as such. That will involve our outer as well as inner worlds.

The next generation has an immense task to master, but how many generations before us haven't also had to experience and overcome great challenges? If our hearts are in the right place, if we have an open attitude to our own shortcomings and mistakes, then we can see the present realistically and regard the future in a positive way.

I think that something good can result from evil and harm if we keep our personal vision of a better world fast in our hearts. Cynicism, often regarded as an integral part of our culture, only brings inertia. Envy and despair are dead ends, and lead to nothing. But when we are optimistic and believe in our abilities and possibilities, then we can move mountains, contribute to positive change in the world, and save the planet. I have hardly ever seen a cynic who contributed to important changes that brought improvement. As far as I can see, great movements that achieve change usually begin with the opposite kind of attitude—that is, with the causal force of "the positive," "power," and "potential."

Life is an exciting journey, and each one of us has the ability to make it beautiful while looking reality straight in the eye along the way. You, Father Anselm, have said: if we carry good and positive images in us and see nature in front of our spiritual eyes, then we can be assured that we are also carrying divine images within ourselves with the vision that God has of our universe.

ANSELM GRÜN: Yes, we need good images within us. And according to Plato, the good images correspond to the picture that God made for himself of each one of us and of our universe. We will become a blessing for this world if we conform with the image of our own character and handle the world as God imagined. God had in mind the picture of a blooming garden that human beings would maintain, with fruits that would please them. But they can only be pleased with it when they do not plunder the garden. If we approach the task of dealing with the world and managing our enterprises with this image offered by the Bible, then we may go into the future full of hope.

I see the situation similarly to you, Mr. Zeitz. Of course I can stare at all the negative developments in our world— at the terrorism, the organized crime, and the greedy financial sharks who can lose an entire national economy on the stock market. But even with all this, I still look at the world with belief and hope. Hope, as St. Paul says, hopes for that which it cannot see. We often don't see the good in people who are only out for money, but I don't allow my belief and hope to be spoiled. I am confident that there is a longing for goodness in every human being, and I see it as my duty to address and awaken this longing.

I believe that the yearning for goodness is stronger than the craving for total destruction. The destructive person has been wounded. He sees violence as the only way to escape his own catastrophic inner mood. But I know plenty of healthy and motivated people. I recently gave a lecture to the students of a business school. I saw so many committed eyes in so many hopeful faces. That makes me still more confident that these people will create a more humane world.

Mr. Zeitz, you and I are stamped by this hope in the same way. We see the world realistically, but we refuse to look at it with dark glasses. We see it through the glasses of confidence and hope. We have faith that we will inflame our readers with our hopeful view of things. We have no patent formula for the solution of the world's problems, but we believe that our thoughts address many people's longings for a different business culture—one that is sustainable, impartial, fair, social, and finally joyful and creative—and encourage them to trust that longing. We trust that we will not only awaken hope in people, but will also weave hope into the world, so that it can be a livable and lovable space for a long time to come.

NOTES

Chapter 1: Success

1. Roger Fisher, William L. Ury, and Bruce M. Patton, *Getting to Yes* (New York: Penguin, 1981).
2. David Strauss, *How to Make Collaboration Work* (San Francisco: Berrett and Koehler, 2002).
3. Peter M. Senge, Bryan Smith, Nina Kruschwitz, Joe Laur, and Sara Schley, *The Necessary Revolution* (New York: Doubleday, 2008).

Chapter 2: Prosperity

1. Lance H. K. Secretan, *Reclaiming Higher Ground: Creating Organizations That Inspire the Soul* (Caledon, Ontario, Canada: The Secretan Center, 1997).

Chapter 3: Culture

1. C. G. Jung, *Dreams* (Princeton, NJ: Princeton University Press, 1974).
2. Edgar Schein, *Organizational Culture and Leadership*, 4th ed. (San Francisco: Jossey-Bass, 2010).

Chapter 5: Acting Ethically

1. Friends of Cameroon, "After First Year, Tested Nonprofit Renews Pledge to Create Jobs In Cameroon" (June 18, 2012). Retrieved from

www.friendsofcameroon.org/2012/06/18/after-first-year-tested-nonprofit-renews-pledge-to-create-jobs-in-cameroon

2. Friedrich Nietzsche, *The Will to Power* (New York: Knopf Doubleday, 1967). Originally published 1883–1886.

Chapter 6: The Environment

1. Wade Davis, *Light at the Edge of the World* (Vancouver, BC: Douglas and McIntyre, 2001).

Chapter 7: Commerce

1. Michael F. Jacobson and Laurie Ann Mazur, *Marketing Madness* (Boulder, CO: Westview Press, 1995).
2. Boyd Cohen and Monika Winn, "Market Imperfections, Opportunity and Sustainable Entrepreneurship," *Journal of Business Venturing* 22 (2007): 29–49.
3. Donella Meadows, *The Limits to Growth* (Signet: New York, 1972).
4. Paul Hawken, Amory B. Lovins, and L. Hunter Lovins, *Natural Capitalism* (Boston: Little, Brown and Company, 1999).
5. Sustainable Apparel Coalition, www.apparelcoalition.org

Chapter 8: Sustainability

1. The film was made possible through financing from the French firm PPR, which has a majority interest in PUMA, and as of 2012 it has been seen by more than five hundred million viewers worldwide.

Chapter 10: Responsibility

1. Lorraine Code, *Epistemic Responsibility* (Providence, RI: Brown University Press, 1987).

Chapter 11: Awareness

1. For an English version, please see Martin Buber, *Tales of the Hasidim* (New York: Schocken, 1991).

ACKNOWLEDGMENTS

I once saw an unusual dedication in a book that read, "To my three small children, without whom I would have finished this book two years earlier." For me, it is like this: without the help of a number of people, I would not have finished my contribution to this book for two *more* years.

Writing a book, or even just half a book, as I have done, is not an easy job for a layman like myself. I admire those who can put together several volumes of outstanding work with ease. For me, writing was a highly interesting but demanding experience, for it was the first time I had picked up a pen since my university years. In addition, I had to write in many different places and do justice to my ongoing professional obligations at the same time.

I would like to use this opportunity to thank those who played a part in the creation of this book, directly or indirectly. This book, like my years of work as CEO of PUMA, would have been impossible without the invaluable support, teamwork, and expertise of the following people:

First of all, sincere thanks to Father Anselm Grün for carrying out this joint project with me. I also wish to thank Abbot Michael and the monks who found time to talk with me during my stay and my numerous visits to the monastery, and particularly Father Mauritius, with his many creative suggestions as publishing director. Professor and coeditor Tom Cooper at Emerson College, Boston, provided most valuable insights and input as well as supporting materials and knowledge in a number of fields. Our U.S. editors Karen Murphy and John Maas made many positive critical suggestions.

My very personal thanks go to Andrea Brenninkmeyer, who carries out excellent work in important social projects in her area, and stimulates many people. She was a source of inspiration for me.

Dr. Ulf Santjer, director of corporate communications at PUMA, also provided valuable support.

I thank those who allowed me to lead the company over the past eighteen years. The board of directors of the company has always supported me, particularly François-Henri Pinault, chairman and CEO of PPR and Thore Ohlsson, who made me CEO of PUMA in 1993. I am appreciative for the support of my employees and both former and present colleagues in management at PUMA over the past two decades until my retirement as CEO last year. They have shown initiative, team spirit, and tremendous commitment. I certainly do not want to forget my former long-time colleague on the board, ally, and special friend Martin Gänsler, who was the first in the company to address ecological issues and express his concerns about them. He took on the subject of sustainability early on.

Finally, thanks must also go to my parents, who have enabled me to become the person I am today. No thanks can be adequate for the decades of their loving support and understanding.

People who contributed but are not named here should be assured that I value them. Unlike that writer whose book would have been finished two years earlier (were it not for his three small children), without all my helpers I would still not be ready to write "Many thanks!"

Jochen Zeitz

I would like to join in with my own thanks. I thank Jochen Zeitz for devoting so much time and dedication to our joint project. I would also like to express my thanks for the hospitality and openness with which he introduced me to his company and the corporate philosophy at Puma. This motivated me to reflect about our own business operations at the abbey.

I wish to thank my fellow brothers and coworkers in those businesses and in the administration with whom I have shared a common path for thirty-four years. It is because of them that I have sufficient time to write books and give lectures because I can count on them to carry out their work in accordance with my wishes, even when I am not on hand.

And, of course, I wish to thank my parents, who gave me that fundamental self-reliance that enables me to engage confidently with my employees and awaken their enthusiasm for work through my faith in them.

Anselm Grün

JOCHEN ZEITZ

Born on April 6, 1963, in Mannheim, Germany, Jochen Zeitz is director of PPR, chairman of the board's sustainable development committee, and cochair and president of The B Team, after having been the CEO of the Sport & Lifestyle division and chief sustainability officer (CSO) of PPR since 2010. Prior to this, Zeitz served for eighteen years as chairman and CEO of PUMA. On being appointed CEO in 1993 at the age of thirty, he transformed the company financially, turning PUMA from a low-priced, undesirable brand with sales of less than two hundred million euros into a desirable, premium company, with sales of three billion euros in 2011 and one of the top three brands in the sporting good industry. He became a member of the board of directors of Harley-Davidson in 2007 and is chair of Harley-Davidson's sustainability committee.

With the goal of bringing business into a new era of corporate, social, and environmental sustainability, Zeitz introduced PUMAVision in 2008. In May 2011 he pioneered an Environmental Profit & Loss Account that puts a monetary value to a business's use of ecosystem services across the entire supply chain.

He also founded the nonprofit Zeitz Foundation of Intercultural Ecosphere Safety in 2008, serves as a board member of Wilderness Safaris, and is a member of the TEEB (The Economics of Ecosystems and Biodiversity) advisory board.

In October 2012, Zeitz cofounded and launched The B Team with Sir Richard Branson to help transform the future of business. It is made up of international CEOs and respected business leaders. The B Team provides a platform to advocate and implement viable and scalable solutions across business sectors.

Zeitz has received numerous awards during his professional career, including "Entrepreneur of the Year," "Trendsetter of the Year," and "Strategist of the Year" by the *Financial Times.* In 2004, the German Federal president awarded him with the Federal Cross of Merit of the Republic of Germany. Due to initiatives that Zeitz implemented, PUMA was given the German Sustainability Award 2010 for "Most Sustainable Strategy" and selected as the "Overall Winner" and the "Biodiversity" winner of the Guardian Sustainable Business Awards 2012, to name but a few. In 2012, PUMA was ranked first in the "Top 10 Global Sustainability Leaders" in the EIRIS' Sustainability Ratings report, and PPR was among Fast Company's "World's 50 Most Innovative Companies" as a result of PPR HOME and "making luxury sustainable."

Zeitz lives in Kenya and Switzerland. Find more information on him at www.facebook.com/zeitzj and via Twitter at @jochenzeitz.

ANSELM GRÜN

Father Anselm Grün, OSB, Th.D., is the Cellarer (financial manager) of the Münsterschwarzach Abbey, near Würzburg, Germany. Since 1977, he has managed approximately three hundred employees. He is recognized as one of the most widely read Christian authors today. He has written more than three hundred books, which have been translated into more than thirty-five languages, selling more than sixteen million copies worldwide. Father Grün also delivers countless courses and talks to address the needs and questions of contemporary life, and serves as the spiritual counselor to many managers. In March 2007 he was awarded the German Federal Cross of Merit and in 2011 received the Bavarian Distinguished Service Award.

Father Grün was born in the Franconian town of Junkershausen and grew up in Munich. At nineteen he became a Benedictine monk at Münsterschwarzach Abbey, learning the art of leading others based on the Rule of St. Benedict of Nursia. He also studied philosophy, theology, and business administration.

INDEX

A

Acting ethically, 65–77; dialogue on, 71–77; models of, 73–75, 99; philosophical and legal guidelines for, 71–73; private organization promoting, 70; PUMA's 4Keys approach to, 66–69; PUMA's history of, 65–66, 69–70; sharing wealth as, 75–77

Adidas, 100

Amos (prophet), 40

Aristotle, 114, 147

Asceticism, 19–20, 115

Authenticity: in monastery, 29, 73, 74; success and, 5; with truthfulness, 60

Awareness, 159–175; competition and, 166–168; dialogue on, 164–175; of global interconnectedness, 164; God and money and, 171–172; of good in world, 173–175; self-awareness, 159–161; from spirituality and religion, 168–171, 172; of weaknesses, 161–163, 164–166

B

Becker, Boris, 151

Being: Buddhism on, 16–17, 170–171; success as, 4–6

Benedict, Pope, 140

Benedict, Saint: on faith, 54; on hearing God's voice, 16; on moderation, 19–20, 21, 22, 52, 115–116; on modesty, 74; on praising God, 81; on seeking God, 73; stability emphasized by, 163; on watching your own

187

189